HARRY LORAYNE'S
PAGE-A-MINUTE
MEMORY BOOK

By Harry Lorayne

Harry Lorayne's Page-a-Minute Memory Book
The Memory Book

HARRY LORAYNE

BALLANTINE BOOKS • NEW YORK

A Ballantine Book
Published by The Random House Publishing Group

Copyright © 1985 by Harry Lorayne, Inc.

All rights reserved.

Published in the United States by Ballantine Books, an imprint of
The Random House Publishing Group, a division of Random
House, Inc., New York, and simultaneously in Canada by Random
House of Canada Limited, Toronto.

Ballantine and colophon are registered trademarks of Random
House, Inc.

www.ballantinebooks.com

Library of Congress Catalog Card Number: 96-96666

ISBN: 978-0-345-41014-6

This edition published by arrangement with Holt, Rinehart and
Winston

Manufactured in the United States of America

First Ballantine Books Mass Market Edition: July 1986
First Ballantine Books Trade Edition: August 1996

146122990

To
Renée and Robert
What lovely, indelible
memories
they've given me

Contents

Introduction

It's always been a matter of wonder to me that people who don't think twice about obtaining eyeglasses to aid failing eyesight, or using a hearing aid to help them hear better, assume that nothing can be done about their "poor" memories. Some become sudden experts on the subject; they emphatically and knowingly state, "I have a lousy memory and that's it!"

Well, hogwash! It's easier to bring your supposedly poor memory to an amazingly high level than it is, in most cases, to alleviate a physical defect.

I became interested in trained-memory systems when I was a schoolboy. My motivation was an obvious one— my father would punish me severely if I received a low grade on a test. I realized that I was getting those low grades for one reason only—I couldn't remember the answers to the test questions. Because, like most children, I didn't have the time or patience to use rote memory; I was too busy playing. So I searched for and found books on memory systems, some dating back to the seventeenth century. At my tender age, I didn't understand seven-eighths of the material in those books. But, oh— that one-eighth! It changed my life.

The first obvious change was the end of punishment by my father, as my grades were no longer low. But most of the ideas I found in those books were old-fashioned and cumbersome. I had to streamline them, making them work in more practical areas like schoolwork. In order to do this, I had to invent some systems of my own. I taught these systems in my first book, which was published in 1957 and became very successful.

After that I wrote more books on the subject, founded the Harry Lorayne School of Memory in New York, ran hundreds of corporate seminars, and demonstrated my memory systems on just about every radio and television show in the country, as well as abroad.

After teaching these systems and techniques for so many years, I've distilled them down to the basics—so that you can start applying them to your memory needs, whatever they may be, instantly. This book, then, offers a new teaching method, specially designed to impart my systems as easily and quickly as possible.

My goal is not to better or improve your memory. "Better" and "improve" are mundane words, not strong enough to convey what really can be done. I want to give you *memory POWER you never imagined possible*— whether you're a student, business executive, or anything in between. And, I want to do it quickly—a "page a minute."

Bear in mind that you aren't reading a novel. You're learning simple systems that will train your memory to an unprecedented degree when you practice and use them. At the start, I'll teach you the basic techniques and principles. Toward the center of the book you'll be applying those techniques in more complex ways. The last part of the book will give you more specific applications, and show how you can adapt these systems to solve every memory problem you will ever face.

Work along with me. Give each page a minute or so (some a bit more, some a bit less), and you'll have a trained memory. You will remember anything you want to (whether you see it, read it, or hear it) faster and better than someone with an IQ of 200!

Trying the ideas is the key. Once you try, you'll be hooked, because you'll see immediate results. You'll see that you can bring your memory to a sharpness and effectiveness that will amaze not only your friends and colleagues but even yourself.

You'll gain an ability that will afford you an edge--one you'll use throughout the rest of your life.

All knowledge is but
remembrance.
                        —*Plato*

You have a fantastic memory.
Want to prove it to yourself?
Okay,
Try to *forget* something
you already know!

ASSOCIATE
You'll
be
Great!

The starting point, the ignition, of memory is association. Association may be subconscious (in other words, uncontrolled) or conscious (in other words, controlled).

Conscious, controlled association
= a trained memory!

> **The Reminder Principle:
> We usually remember one
> thing because we are
> *reminded* of it by another
> thing.**

There is no way you could count the number of times you
have looked at, heard, or thought of one thing and it made
you say or think, "Oh, that reminds me..." (of another
thing). Your mind snapped its fingers!

> **The reminder principle is a
> natural phenomenon.**

Our minds work that way naturally. Consider the standard
"association" tests, as in, "I'll say a word; you say the
first word that comes to your mind." An obvious example:
I say "black," you answer "white."
Most of us would automatically say:

down	when we hear	up
cold	when we hear	hot
wrong	when we hear	right
summer	when we hear	winter
day	when we hear	night
no	when we hear	yes
little	when we hear	big
out	when we hear	in

Many times, the thing that makes your mind snap its fingers seems to have nothing to do with the thing it reminds you of.

Ah, but it does. You simply aren't aware of it.

Association is the best way there is to make you aware of it—to make that reminder principle work for you, whenever you want it to. That is, if you can *control* these associations.

So what exactly *is* association?

> **Association is simply the mental connecting or binding together of two "things."**

That's all. And *only* two things—always. Association is an easy mental act or effort. A *reminder-connection.*

These mental acts or efforts not only enable you to acquire a memory you never thought possible, they also give you a much better sense of observation, concentration, imagination, and confidence. They make you a more alert, more aware human being.

Interest

One of the spark plugs of memory is interest. It is *always* easier to remember things you're interested in than to remember things you're *not* interested in.

Lee Iacocca says (in *Fortune* magazine, August 1978) that he believes that memory depends mainly on interest. "If you care, you remember." He makes *mental lists* every morning of the things he wants to accomplish that day.

The point is this: Mental reminder-connections *force* you to be *interested* in those "things" at that moment!

Association forces interest.

> **In order to remember any new thing, it must be associated to something we already know or already remember.**

After two things are associated, the thing you already know *reminds* you of the new thing—and it continues to do so until the new thing *becomes* something you already know.

Never beLIEve a LIE

This sentence is a good example of an association that will always help you to remember that the word "believe" is spelled beLIEve, not beLEIve. I'm making an assumption here—that you already know how to spell "lie," and that the spelling of "believe" is the problem.

Think of that sentence—Never beLIEve a LIE—and you've made something you already *know* (the spelling of "lie") help you remember a new thing (the spelling of "believe").

The same idea will work for "piece"—a PIEce of PIE. Or for "balloon"—a BALLoon is shaped like a BALL (two l's in "balloon"). Or, to intERRupt is to ERR.

The same idea applies when remembering the correct spellings of similar words:

To be stationAry is to stAnd still.

To use stationEry is to writE a lEtter.

I'll discuss spelling problems a bit more
on pages 128–129.

As a schoolboy I had trouble spelling the word "rhythm" correctly. I must have spelled it twelve different ways— all wrong. Finally, I thought of the phrase "*R*ed *H*ot, *Y*ou *T*wo-*H*eaded *M*onster."

"Red hot," in those days, was a popular expression for fast-tempo music. I *pictured* a two-headed drummer and thought of that phrase.

To this day I have to stop for a beat before I type or write "rhythm." However, I no longer misspell it (haven't since I was a schoolboy) because I still think "Red Hot, You Two-Headed Monster"!

In simple ways, teachers have been applying the basic memory rule of association for years. Remember "Every Good Boy Does Fine"? That's how your music teacher taught you to remember notes on the bars of the treble clef.

How is it that most of us know the shape of Italy, whereas few can recall the shape of England or France? It's because back in elementary school, a teacher taught us to associate the shape of Italy with a shape we were already familiar with—a boot.

Associations triggered by acronyms work on the same principle. Medical students have used these associations for years to help them remember the facts they need to pass their exams. A fairly easy one is for the layers of the scalp:

S—skin
C—close connective tissue; cutaneous vessels and nerves
A—aponeurosis (epicranial)
L—loose connective tissues
P—pericranium

Such an acronym can also help you with nontechnical things. Visualize (see in your mind's eye) many *HOMES* on a *great lake*. *HOMES* will remind you of the names of the five Great Lakes: Huron, Ontario, Michigan, Erie, and Superior.

> **If it can be visualized, it can be easily remembered.**

The problem is that some of us have trouble visualizing. Association aids visualization. When you associate one thing to another properly, it's difficult *not* to visualize those two things.

The "things" could be anything—name, face, number, appointment, word, foreign word, fact—anything. Don't let the word or the concept of "visualization" throw you. It's something you've been doing all your life. When you think, you see pictures in your mind—that's visualization. Aristotle said it in one of his books on memory:

> *"In order to think, we must speculate*
> *with images."*

Think of, say, a zebra. Don't you *see* that black-and-white striped horselike animal in your mind's eye? Of course you do—and that's all I mean by "visualize." All my systems are based on *natural* phenomena.

How does association aid visualization? Let's say I told you to see a zebra behind the teller's cage at your bank. When you think of *teller*, you will visualize a zebra (cashing a check, perhaps), and vice versa. *One makes you visualize the other.*

When my son, Robert, was about five years old, he was frustrated because he could never remember to say "caterpillar" but instead always said "caterlipper." I told him to picture a *cat* chasing that crawly, hairy thing up a *pillow*. It worked.

Let's Start with Words

Peduncle means flower stalk.

If you had to, or wanted to, how could you remember that? You'd associate the new "thing," peduncle, to the "thing" you already know—flower stalk.

A problem of a different color arises here. How do you visualize a word like *peduncle*? Well, make it meaningful, tangible, so that it *can* be visualized. Listen to the word. It sounds like "paid uncle." And, the phrase "paid uncle" is meaningful and, just as important, it will *remind* you of peduncle. Most importantly, it can also, now, be connected to—associated to—flower stalk.

For example, visualize this: You owe your uncle money; you *paid uncle* with flower stalks instead of money. Seems silly? Who cares. It *works!* This simple association will work left-right and right-left. If you hear or think of flower stalk, that will *remind* you of paid uncle—peduncle. If you hear or think of peduncle, that will remind you of paid uncle—flower stalk.

The more intelligible a thing is, the more easily it is retained in the memory, and contrariwise, the less intelligible it is, the more easily we forget it.
—Benedict Spinoza

The
Substitute
Word
System

> **Seemingly abstract and intangible "things" *can* be visualized and, therefore, associated.**

All you have to do is think of something that sounds like that word—enough to remind you of it. This is *The Substitute Word System* of memory. A Substitute Word, phrase, or thought is used to enable you to visualize the under-ordinary-circumstances abstract "thing."

That's the system you used to remember the pronunciation *and* the meaning of *peduncle*. A phrase that *could* be visualized—paid uncle—enabled you to visualize an abstract word.

More Words

An *endocarp* is a fruit pit. Picture (visualize) yourself hitting a carp (fish) with a gigantic *fruit pit*. This is the *end o' the carp*. Sure, it's silly, but try it—just see that crazy picture in your mind for a second.

You see, I *want* the mental "picture" to be silly or ridiculous or bizarre or illogical or impossible. This not only helps you form the association-picture—it also forces you to apply the "slap in the face" principle.

Basic Idea: If you received a slap in the face just as you were told a piece of important information, you'd most likely *never forget* that particular piece of information. But a slap in the face hurts. The ridiculous-picture idea achieves the same thing painlessly. It helps form a strong, lasting association because it brings your mind into focus.

It enables you to grab your mind by the scruff of its neck and tell it—force it—to *pay attention*. And, said Samuel Johnson:

"The true art of memory is the art of attention."

> **The silliness of the image automatically brings the "slap in the face" principle into play.**

As it does with these examples:

Litany—a form of prayer.

Visual mental image: You've set fire to one of your knees (lit a knee) and you're saying a *prayer* over that lit knee.

"See" that silly picture and you'll never forget that word and its meaning. ("Lit Annie" would do as well.)

Do you see that the visual picture—the association—embraces the *two* vital entities? It embraces the new "thing"—the word you want to remember—and its definition or meaning.

Piebald—having patches of black and white; particolored.

Visual image: A gigantic pie with a bald head (pie bald—piebald) is covered with black and white patches, or is parti-colored.

See that silly picture in your mind's eye.

The "Slap in the Face" Principle

If you walked out of your office and a few drops of rain splattered onto you, you would quickly forget it ever happened. If, however, buckets of water poured over your head, soaking you—you would remember the event and probably recount it in detail for years.

If you stopped to rest in a meadow and a cow or two wandered by, you might enjoy that pleasant moment—but would quickly forget it. If a crazed bull came into that meadow and you had to run for your life—you'd *never* forget it.

You see hundreds of cars each day and rarely pay attention. If you saw one man picking up a car and walking off with it, you'd never forget it.

Most people remember exactly where they were and what they were doing when they first heard the news of President John Kennedy's assassination, and that happened many years ago.

That's the basis of the "slap in the face" principle.

Why not take advantage of this natural phenomenon? We tend to forget the simple, mundane, everyday, ordinary things. We rarely forget the unique, the violent, the unusual, the absurd, the extraordinary. Make your associations unusual, ridiculous, impossible—and they'll stick like burrs.

Rorqual—a type of whale.
Mental image, or association: You use a raw quill to kill a whale. Or you roar as you kill a whale. (Raw quill, roar kill—rorqual.)

Now—do you know what an endocarp is?
What's a peduncle?
A litany?
A rorqual?

See if you can learn these words the way I've taught you—this time on your own.

Probity—integrity; honesty
Sambar—deer with pointed antlers
Orlop—lowest deck of a ship
Anchorite—a hermit
Olfactory—pertaining to the sense of smell
Flippant—glib, impertinent, disrespectful
Peruke—a wig
Omphalos—the navel (perhaps "arm fall loose." Falls where? Into the *navel*, of course!)

You're Using Your
IMAGINUITY

A bit of *imagin*ation plus a bit of inge*nuity*.

Imagination can be more important than knowledge. What good is knowledge if you don't have the imagination to *use* it!?

MEMORY BREAK #1

Do you think you can remember—learn—ten pairs of "things"? You can, if I give you a memory aid for each. We'll start with two pairs.

Let 1 = T, D. What I want you to remember is that the number or digit *1* will be *represented by the sound* made by the letters T or D. And vice versa. (The letter D makes the *same* sound as a T; it's a bit softer is all.)

Let 2 = n. The number or digit 2 will be *represented by the sound* made by the letter n, and vice versa.

I realize, of course, that you don't know why you're remembering this. Take my word for it—you'll be glad you did.

Here's a memory aid to help you remember that T = 1: The letter T can be formed with a pair of 1's. The first forms the stem; the other forms the crossbar. Or—a typewritten T has *one* downstroke.

To remember that n = 2: The typewritten small n has *two* downstrokes.

Think of those memory aids for a moment, and you'll *know* that T, D = 1; 1 = T, D; n = 2; 2 = n.

To Remember OAR Not to Remember

The systems you're learning and applying are means to an end. The visual images you form, the associations, will not linger in your mind forever. You'll be amazed at how quickly they fade.

They're needed only *at first*—to help you impress or register new information in your mind in the first place; I refer to this as "original awareness." Once that information is registered via an appropriate reminder-connection, your memory automatically stores the word or information correctly *as it was originally registered.* Therefore, if you visualize, say, an arm falling loose into the navel to recall "omphalos," you needn't worry that you'll come up with, say, "armphaloos" instead.

Thomas De Quincey wrote:

"I feel assured that there is no such thing as ultimate forgetting; traces once impressed upon the memory are indestructible."

Anything that is impressed—*registered in the first place*—is usually easily remembered or recalled.

The problem has always been to impress or register new information in the first place.

Forming an association forces you to register the information—at that time. It forces you to pay attention to— to *observe*—that information.

Call it the OAR method:

<u>O</u>bserve
<u>A</u>ssociate
<u>R</u>emember

> **Even if the systems don't
> work—they must work!**

That sounds ridiculous, but it's true.

And here's why: Simply making the slight effort to think up a Substitute Word for the seemingly intangible word you want to remember—and forming an association—forces initial observation, registering, and remembering. It forces *attention*.

So, even if the techniques don't work—which they most definitely do—you're concentrating on that new "thing" as you've never done before. You're *registering* that information automatically by *trying* to apply the systems. You'll be strengthening your memory whether or not the systems work!

You have been using the Substitute Word System to help you remember unfamiliar English words. An English word that's new to you is as intangible as a word from a foreign language. That should lead you to believe that you can apply exactly the same idea to foreign language vocabulary. You're absolutely right!

As a matter of fact, it's one of the most fascinating, and rewarding, applications of my systems.

Ordinarily, if you heard the French word for watermelon—*pastèque*—and wanted to remember it, you'd have to go over it and over it—repetition, boredom—and hope it would work.

All you have to do now is form a silly association between "pass deck" and watermelon! Perhaps you're playing cards with a big watermelon and you ask it to *pass* the *deck* to you. Or, you're playing cards with watermelons *instead of* cards, and another player passes the deck (a stack of watermelons).

Foreign Language Vocabulary

The French word for bridge is *pont*.

It sounds like *punt*. "See" yourself *punt*ing a football completely over a bridge. Or, you're punting a bridge instead of a football.

The French word for father is *père*. See a gigantic *pear* (the fruit) rocking you (or a baby) in its arms.

The French word for cork is *bouchon*. "Push on" is a good reminder or Substitute Word. See yourself mightily *push*ing *on* a gigantic cork, trying to get it into a wine bottle.

The Swedish word for trousers is *bygsor* (pronounced beek soar). Picture a gigantic pair of pants (just the pants; no one in 'em) with a *big sore*. (A bird's *beak* that's *sore* would also do.)

The Japanese word for goodbye—*sayonara*—would be so easy to remember if you visualize yourself *sigh*ing *on air* as you say goodbye.

The French word for grapefruit is *pamplemousse*. See large yellow *pimples* all over a *moose*; each pimple is really a grapefruit.

Up a Creek—With an OAR

If you've tried to *see* those pictures in your mind's eye you have automatically *O*bserved, *A*ssociated, and *R*emembered.

See if it isn't so: What's the French word for watermelon? (Don't worry about spelling.)

For bridge?

For father?

For cork?

What's the Swedish word for trousers?

The Japanese word *sayonara* means _____?

What's the French word for grapefruit?

Did you remember these? Of course you did. You're already remembering better than you ever did before.

You've taken foreign words—conglomerations of sound, really—and turned them into meaningful "things" in order to associate them to their English equivalents. You could remember, say, an Italian menu easily, if you wanted to. For example:

Calamari—squid. You *collar* a girl named *Mary* (collar Mary—*calamari*) and force her to eat squid.

Aglio (pronounced al-yo)—garlic. Many people smell of garlic. You say to them. "*All you* people cook with garlic."

Pollo—chicken. Visualize a gigantic chicken playing *polo*.

Vitello—veal. Picture a large letter *V* *tell*ing a large letter *O* (V tell O) about a restaurant that serves only veal.

Dolci—sweets (dessert). Associate *dole she* (or *gee*) or *doll she* (or *gee*) to sweets. (Ain't she sweet?!)

Burro—butter. You're smearing butter all over a *burro* (donkey).

Carpaccio—thin raw beef. You're using thin (pounded) raw beef to put a *patch* on your *car*. The patches might be shaped like an *E* and an *O* (car patch E O).

Verdi—green (as in green vegetables). *Where D* sounds enough like the Italian word to remind you of it. See that *D* being green.

Agnello—lamb. A girl named *Ann* turns *yellow* (Ann yellow) because she's eating too much lamb (or too many lamb chops).

Go over these; form the associations; *see* those pictures. Then test yourself. You'll be pleasantly surprised.

I Recall...

Years ago, a woman brought her twelve-year-old son to one of my courses. She was quite nervous and didn't know whether I could help him—it seems he couldn't remember *any* of his schoolwork. The tuition fee was a lot of money for her, and her husband was against the whole thing.

The father came to pick up the son after one session. It was the session during which I taught how to remember foreign language vocabulary. The father was impatient; he kept sticking his head inside the classroom. At one point he overheard a part of my example of *pample-mousse*—grapefruit—pimple-moose, and I saw a skeptical smirk come over his face.

I'm used to dealing with skeptics; I've done so all my life. I made sure the son learned all the words—and I taught more than usual during that session.

The reason I recall it so clearly: I had the boy and his father stay for a few minutes after the rest of the class left. It was lovely to watch the father's skeptical smirk change to a look of shock as the boy rattled off fifty French words and English meanings that he'd heard for the first time only an hour before!

MEMORY BREAK #2

T = ?
n = ?
Let's learn two more of those pairs.

Let 3 = m.　　　A typewritten small letter m has 3 downstrokes. Or—turn an m on its side, and it looks like a 3.

Let 4 = R.　　　The last sound in the word "fouR" is R.

You should know these before you go to the next page:

$$1 = T, D$$

$$2 = n$$

$$3 = m$$

$$4 = R$$

Observation Without Pain

It's obvious that there's no way to remember anything unless it's observed first. (Remember OAR: Observe, Associate, Remember.) My trained-memory systems and techniques *force* you to observe—without pain, automatically, better than you ever did before—and anything clearly observed is already half memorized.

Too many of us *see* but rarely really observe—and observing is much more important than seeing. If you don't believe that your sense of observation needs sharpening, let me try to prove that it does. Try to answer these questions:

Which traffic light is on top, red or green?

What is the exact balance in your checking account?

Which two letters are *not* on the telephone dial?

Is the number six on your watch face the Arabic figure 6, or the Roman numeral VI?

What color socks are you wearing right now?

If you answered even one of those questions incorrectly, you haven't been observing properly. To look or see is easy; to observe *accurately* is a skill that can be acquired. In the business world, memory and observation can help yield money-making and money-saving ideas and improvements. The effectiveness of most actions, in business and social life, depends to a large extent on your capacity for sharp, thorough, and accurate observation, along with a quick and retentive memory.

Here's the key: We see with our eyes but observe with our *minds*. The difference between seeing with only your eyes and observing (seeing) with your mind is—*attention*. The first, and only, rule for sharpening your sense of observation is *Pay Attention!*

You can acquire a much sharper, keener sense of observation with just a bit of effort; better observation can become a habit if practiced consciously and conscientiously. Observation implies a *clear mental picture* of what is seen in all its detail. Applying the memory systems is the best way to improve your listening and observing facilities.

Get into the habit of asking questions. Let your mind wonder, be curious about things you see, and that seeing will turn to observing. Ask yourself questions about anything you observe. That will arouse your curiosity, and when that's aroused, you're interested; and when you're interested you must observe better and with more accuracy.

There are some specific practice methods for observation. Police rookies are trained to look for and observe certain clues. They learn that people who have calluses on their middle fingers may do a lot of writing, by hand. Finger and palm calluses may tell them that the person is, say, a florist or a seamstress. Shoulder marks may indicate a mail carrier; chin and finger marks, a musician. Rookies train themselves; they *practice* looking for and observing these things. They practice observing characteristic odors of certain professions—bartenders, butchers, medical personnel, grocers.

You, too, can practice observation. Try this: Think of a close friend. Now, using pen and paper, try to describe that person's face in detail. Complete detail. Describe the forehead: Is it high, wide, low, bulging, receding, narrow, lined? Describe the eyes: Color, size, protruding, sunken, close-set, wide-set, type of glasses, any peculiarities? Describe the eyebrows: Slanting, bushy, sparse, normal, plucked, arched, horizontal, connected, thick, thin, color?

Move down the face mentally: Ears, nose, lips, mouth, teeth, chin, mustache. Try to describe each feature in complete, minute detail.

When you see that friend, check your description. Notice (observe) now what you never noticed before, or where you were incorrect. Add these things to your description. Try the same thing with other friends, or perhaps acquaintances. The more you try it, the better your observation will become. Try describing the entire person, not just the face. When you're more proficient, try looking at a stranger's face and describing it later. The more you look with *conscious intention* to observe, the more you will observe each time you try it. Your observation will improve with use and practice.

Here's another way to practice observation: Leave the room you're in right now. That's right! Leave the room. Try to describe the room you just left in complete detail, including position of chairs, lamps, ashtrays, pictures. How many are there of each? Include colors of items, size, and so on. How many windows, size and type of doors, hardware, type of curtains, drapes, shades? Location of telephone, TV set, radio, furniture? List everything you can think of without looking into the room.

Now check. Notice (observe) all the things you *didn't* list, the items that never registered in your mind, that were never really observed. Now, do it all over again. Your list will be much longer each time. Do the same with other rooms. Keep this up, stay with it, and you'll get into the habit of looking with conscious intention to observe—your sense of observation *has to* improve.

Another practice method: Think of a familiar street, one you've walked on many times. Try to list all the stores and businesses on that street (street level). Try listing them in proper sequence. Then check your list. You'll be looking at that street with conscious intention to observe. Try it again—your list will grow longer and more accurate each time you try it.

Look into a store-window display for a short time. Then try to list everything displayed. Try identifying year, make, and model of passing cars at a glance (as policemen do).

Any, or all, of these practice suggestions *must* sharpen your observation, if you try them, if you stick with it. The more you test your observation, the better and harder it will work for you. The more you look and listen with conscious intention to observe—with attention and awareness—the sharper, more accurate, and more efficient your observation will be.

It is important to work on your observation as I've explained, but as soon as you *apply* the actual memory systems I'm teaching you, you'll *automatically* be using and sharpening your observation. In order to apply the systems you have no choice but to be interested, no choice but to look at things with conscious intention to observe.

Apply the memory systems and you *will* be practicing to observe—automatically, and without pain.

THE MOST UNIVERSAL MEMORY COMPLAINT...

I'm introduced to someone,
and a few minutes later—
no, seconds later—
I've forgotten his or her name!

...IS A LIE

It's a lie because you haven't *forgotten* the name. What you did was—you *didn't remember it in the first place.*

You probably didn't even *hear it* in the first place!

You've got to *get* something before you can *for*get it.

The other cliché is: "Oh, I know your face, but I can't remember your name." I've never heard anyone say—"I know your name, but I forgot your face!"

Most of us remember faces—because we've seen them. Names are the problem because we only hear them (if we listen). We remember what we see better than what we hear.

I'll teach you a way to force yourself to "get" the name in the first place.

Names

Before I get to the actual systems, here are five rules that will definitely enhance your ability to remember names.

    1. *Say* the name when you say "hello." (You *have* to hear it in order to do that. Ask for it again, if you haven't heard it.)
    2. Try to *spell* the name. (It doesn't matter if you spell it incorrectly. The person will correct you and be flattered that you care.)
    3. Make a *remark* about the name. (Anything— you never heard a name like it, or it's the same as a friend's name, or it's a lovely name, and so forth.)
    4. *Use* the name during your initial conversation. (Don't overdo it. Just use it a few times where and when it fits.)
    5. *Use* the name when you leave. (Always say "So long, Mr. Smith." Don't just say "So long.")

While these rules are effective and easy to apply, starting on the next page you'll learn the system that makes the above seem like kid stuff.

You can visualize names like Butler, Wolfe, Carpenter, Paige, Forrest, Brooks, Rivers, and so forth, because they already have meanings that allow you to conjure up pictures in your mind. But what about names like Carruthers, Bentavagnia, Ponchatrane, Tropeano, Harrison, Smith, Gardner, Cohen, Sitron, Swanson, Rafferty, Krakowitz— the vast majority of names that have no meaning?

You should know the answer. Apply my Substitute Word (phrase, or thought) System. Think of something that sounds enough like the name to *remind* you of it. Then, you'll have a meaningful "thing" to reminder-connect to that person's face.

But there's more to it. Remember I said that even if the systems don't work, they must work. This is a good example of just that. There's no way you can apply the Substitute Word System without *hearing the name first.* That's half the battle—you're forced to hear that name when you try to apply the system! So, even if the system itself didn't work (which it does), you'd still remember more names than you ever did before.

Zip Names

Mr. Antesiewicz was one of my first students. I call difficult-seeming names like this "zip" names. They go in one ear and *zip* right out the other! Most people simply won't bother trying to properly hear a name like this. They think, "What's the point? I'll never remember it anyway!"

But look: That name is pronounced "ante-sevage." If after you've heard it, you think *anti savage* or *auntie save itch*, it no longer seems so formidable. Suddenly it's meaningful; at the moment, more meaningful than Jones, and therefore *easier to remember* than Jones.

Cameron—camera on
Bentavagnia—a bent (weather) vane can be visualized. Bentavagnia cannot. And "bent vane" is all the reminder you'd need.
Ponchatrane—punch a train
Tropeano—throw piano
Carruthers—car udders
Smith—a blacksmith, or his hammer
Gardner—gardener
Sitron—sit run
Rafferty—rap for tea
Cohen—ice cream cone
Swanson—swan (and) son
Harrison—hairy son

Pukczyva seems like one of those "zip" names until you *listen* and realize that it's pronounced "puck-shiva." Thinking of a hockey *puck shiver*ing "unzips" that name!

There is *no* name, no matter how long, foreign sounding, or strange sounding, to which the Substitute Word System cannot be applied.

I could list a thousand of the most commonly used surnames in America plus my Substitute Word for each. But it's unnecessary—you're better off thinking up your own Substitute Word or phrases. Doing it yourself helps to pinpoint your concentration even more.

Papadopoulos—Papa (father) topple us.
Dimitriades—the meat tree ate E's.

Substitute thoughts like black*smith* (for Smith), cone (for Cohen or Cohn), garden (for Gordon), gardener (for Gardner), become *standards*—thoughts or pictures you'll use for those names without having to take the time or effort to think about it. The same is true for familiar suffixes or prefixes to names.

"Mc" or "Mac"—picture a Mack truck
"Witz" or "itz"—picture brains (wits), or itch
"Ler"—picture a judge's gavel: law
"Son"—son or sun
"Berg"—iceberg
"Stein"—beer stein
"Ly" or "ley"—lea (a meadow)

It isn't essential for your Substitute Word or picture to encompass *every* sound in the name. Remember, all you want or need is a reminder.

Try these yourself—then check your Substitute Words or phrases against mine (on the next page).

Halperin	Costello
Latimore	Smolenski
Cherofski	Fleming
Kusak	Morales
Streicher	Jeffries

Halperin—help her in
Latimore—ladder more
Cherofski—sheriff ski
Kusak—cue sack
Streicher—strike her
Costello—cost hello
Smolenski—small lens ski
Fleming—flaming; lemming
Morales—more or less
Jeffries—Jeff frees; Jeff freeze; chef frees, or freeze

There are always other ways to go—for Streicher, you may have thought of *strike car* or *striped car*. For Kusak—cue sick; Fleming—flame ink; Morales—more alleys; Smolenski—smile and ski; and they'd work just fine.

I've been asked (only by those who have not as yet tried this technique), "Why won't I think that the name is Smolskilens rather than Smolenski if I form the above association?" The answer is that it's your *true* memory that's really doing the work.

All your true memory needs to do its work
is a little reminder.

MEMORY BREAK #3

Two more of those pairs to learn:

Let 5 = L. The Roman numeral for 50 is L. Or, hold up your left hand, palm facing out, 4 fingers together, thumb straight to the right, as if signalling "Stop." The 5 fingers look like the letter L.

Let 6 = J, sh, ch, soft g.

Don't let the many letters throw you. They all make the *same* consonant sound. Not exactly perhaps, but your lips, tongue, teeth are in the same positions when forming those sounds. Here's your memory-aid, which you need only at first: With a slight stretch of the imagination, a capital J is almost the mirror image of a 6.

1	= T, D	4	= R
2	= n	5	= L
3	= m	6	= J, sh, ch, soft g

Know these before you continue. You'll know why you're learning them later on in the book.

And Faces

It is the common wonder of all men, how among so many millions of faces there should be none alike.

— Sir Thomas Browne

When you *look*—that's the key word—at any face, there is usually *one* feature on that face that you notice first.

That one feature will serve as the second "thing" in this important entity of two—name and face.

You've just been introduced to Mr. Bentavagnia. You've listened to the name because you want to think of a Substitute Word or phrase, like *bent vane*. And then you notice his *large nose*.

You may not realize that in order to notice the large nose, you've had to look at his entire face. I'll be teaching you to select one *outstanding feature* on a new person's face. If you simply try to do that one-second mental calisthenic, you'll be forcing yourself to see the entire face.

In truth, which feature you select—nose, ears, lips, chin, hairline, bald head, cheeks, eyes, cleft, wart, pimple, dimple, forehead, eyebrows, wrinkles, creases—is immaterial. You're forced to *look* at the face in order to select it!

Okay; you've "locked in"—decided on—Mr. Bentavagnia's nose.

You've done the two things that the myriad people who complain, "I'm introduced to someone, and seconds later I've forgotten his or her name," do not do. You've *listened* (to the name—you had to in order to come up with *bent vane*) and *looked* (at the face—you had to in order to select an outstanding feature).

Do *nothing* more than this with every new person you meet, and you *must* better your memory for names and faces to a degree you never dreamed possible.

Most of us are mentally lazy. It's easier for some to dig ditches than to think. As has been said, "If you make someone think he's thinking, he'll love you. If you really make him think, he'll hate you."

We must be forced, without pain, to do certain things. The Substitute Word System *forces* you to listen to the name, and the outstanding-feature idea *forces* you to look at the face.

But—you can do something more!

You can lock in the two "things" with a reminder-connection, an association, so that one will remind you of the other.

Look at Mr. Bentavagnia's face, as you shake hands, and visualize a *bent vane* on his face where his *large nose* should be!

You can use pictures for practice. Pictures from newspapers and magazines are fine. Make up names, christen the face-pictures with them, and apply the system. You'll remember the names of the face-pictures.

However, you'll get the same practice when applying the system to *real* faces. You'll be practicing and *accomplishing* at the same time!

One elderly woman told me she'd learned this system because she had quite a few grandchildren and had started to forget their names. But she also practiced on others— neighborhood service people, cashiers, waiters and waitresses, plumber, baker, and so on—until she became a local celebrity, almost a legend, in her suburban neighborhood. Everyone knew her by name because she knew everyone by name!

That's All You Have to Do.

1. Form a Substitute Word, phrase, or thought that will remind you of the name. (The same applies for a first name.)
2. Find one outstanding feature on the face.
3. Associate the two things.

What a simple program for solving the universal memory problem!

And it sure does solve it. I'm probably the best proof of that. Have you ever *seen* Dale Carnegie win friends and influence people? Have you ever *seen* Evelyn Wood read fast—or at all? I don't know anyone who has!

But millions have seen me remember the names and faces of up to 700 people after quickly meeting them once, on just about every national television show and at corporate speaking engagements.

You also may have seen my students demonstrate their ability to remember names and faces on television. More important, people all over the world apply, use, and *benefit from* the systems.

A year before I first went on the Ed Sullivan show, a friend was telling Ed what I do: I have everyone in the audience stand, and then when I call a person's name, he or she sits down—until I've seated all 400–500 people. But my friend was a bit "off sync" in his explanation and told Ed that people would *stand up* when I pointed and called out names. Said Mr. Sullivan, "I can have my orchestra play 'The Star-Spangled Banner' and get the same effect!"

How Do You Do, Mr. Pukczyva?

You've thought of puck-shiver and, as you shake hands, you notice the obvious cleft in his chin. *Lock it in.* See one (or many) hockey pucks flying out of that cleft; they're all shivering.

Mr. Brodsky: You think "broad ski." He has deep lines on his forehead. See *broad skis* skiing on those lines.

Miss Ponchatrane: She has large ears. See trains coming out of those ears; you're *punch*ing *a train.*

Mr. Papadopoulos: He has a very wide mouth. See a donkey (ass) coming out of that mouth. Your father (Papa) pushes over—*topples*—the *ass. (Papa topple ass.)*

Mr. Robrum: He has bushy eyebrows. See a bottle of rum over each eye (instead of eyebrows) and you're *rob*bing the *rum.*

Mrs. Smith: She has deep lines from nostrils to the corners of her mouth. You're pounding those lines deeper with a black*smith*'s hammer.

Mr. Carruthers: He has a very high forehead. See cars driving across that forehead; the *cars* have *udders* (like a cow)—you're milking the cars.

Mr. Kusak: He has wide bulging eyes. See *cue* sticks flying out of those eyes—into a *sack.*

Do these associations seem silly? Good. I want them to be silly. I'm result-oriented; I care only whether an idea works or not. Will this idea help you remember names and faces better than you thought possible?

Yes—it will!

‖ 45 ‖

Apply the System

Starting now! Apply it when meeting one new person, or when you're introduced to a few new people in a group. What can you lose? The worst that can happen is that it won't work and you'll forget names. So what? You've been doing that all your life!

Are you wondering whether you can use, say, the nose over and over with different people? Yes, you can; it won't matter. You can also use the same Substitute Word for different people—if it fits.

What if you can't find an outstanding feature? This will rarely happen; there are few perfect faces. But, in order to decide that there's no outstanding feature, you had to look and that's what's most important. Then, use *any* feature.

My guarantee: After you try to apply the system *three* separate times, you'll be remembering 100 percent more names and faces than you ever did.

There's method to my madness. The only way you can prove me wrong is by trying to apply the system *at least* three times!

By that time, I guarantee you'll be a convert.

Recap

So far, you've seen that the key to a better memory is that *information must register in the first place*. Most often, when we say we "forget" something, we really haven't forgotten it. What we did is not *remember* it in the first place.

Association, forming silly mental pictures, *forces* us to register information in the first place.

OAR—Observe, Associate, Remember.

You've applied the ideas to help you remember new English and foreign words and their meanings, and to remember unfamiliar names and faces. You've learned how to make an intangible group of sounds meaningful by applying the Substitute Word System.

You've also learned, although you still don't know why, that:

1 = T, D	4 = R
T, D = 1	R = 4
2 = n	5 = L
n = 2	L = 5
3 = m	6 = J, sh, ch, soft g
m = 3	J, sh, ch, soft g = 6

The
Link
System

I doubt that anyone with an untrained memory can possibly remember twenty items in sequence after hearing or seeing them only once. You will be able to do that—and more—after you read and study this section.

First, I want you to remember these eight items *in sequence*!

Pen, shoe, book, airplane, eyeglasses, fish, Benadryl, typewriter.

Don't panic! Go to the next page.

The eight items in the list could be your appointment/ errands for tomorrow; they could be the eight thoughts of your speech or sales talk. At the moment, what they represent is immaterial. I just made them up. What is material is that, now, with what you've already learned, you can remember them in sequence, easily. Because each of the "things" already has meaning (one is a bit "iffy"), each can be visualized and associated.

Start by picturing a pen. That's all. Perhaps a familiar pen, or an expensive pen you own, or any pen.

Now, simply make the assumption that you already know *pen*. The problem is the "new" thing—the shoe. But in order to remember any new thing, it must be associated *in a ridiculous way* to something you already know. Since you already know *pen* and the new thing is shoe, you can apply that rule.

Form a silly or impossible picture, association, or reminder-connection between pen and shoe. Although there are many choices, all you need is *one* picture. You can see yourself wearing gigantic pens instead of shoes, or writing with a shoe instead of a pen, or you can see millions of pens flying out of a shoe, and so on. Select one, and *see* that picture in your mind's eye.

You'll see how well this works only if you try it!

If you've seen the picture between pen and shoe, stop thinking about it now. Go to the next association, which is *shoe* to *book*. At this moment, the assumption is that you already know shoe, so that can be made to remind you of the new thing—book.

Select one of the following pictures, or one you think of yourself, and *see* it in your mind's eye for a second or so.

You're wearing large books instead of shoes; a large shoe is reading a book; a book is wearing shoes and walking; you open a book and millions of shoes fly out and kick you in the face.

Any one of these is fine. An "instead of" picture is usually easiest to come up with—at least it is for me. Seeing one of the items larger than life (gigantic) or seeing millions of the same item helps to make the picture silly or illogical. So does action—walking, or being hit in the face, and so forth.

If you've visualized the action between shoe and book, stop thinking about it now. Proceed to the next association.

Form an association or reminder-connection between *book* and *airplane*. You might see a gigantic book flying like an airplane, millions of books boarding an airplane, a large book flying an airplane. *See* the picture you select.

Now, *airplane* to *eyeglasses*. You can use the same idea—a large pair of eyeglasses flying like an airplane; millions of eyeglasses boarding an airplane, and so on. Or, you're wearing airplanes instead of eyeglasses; an airplane is wearing gigantic eyeglasses. *See* the picture you've selected. (Usually, the first silly picture that comes to mind will suffice.)

Eyeglasses to *fish*. Obvious! A fish is wearing eyeglasses. Or, millions of eyeglasses are swimming like fish, or you're wearing a fish over each eye instead of eyeglasses.

Don't go to the next page until you've *seen* that picture in your mind.

Fish to *Benadryl*. I stuck in "Benadryl" to make you stop and think for only a moment. Benadryl is a drug for allergies and, ordinarily, how would you associate fish (or anything) to that name? It ordinarily can't be visualized. But now you know that it can be visualized. Use a Substitute Word or phrase. "Bend a drill" will do it—it's certainly enough to remind you of Benadryl.

So, you might see a gigantic fish bending a drill; a bent drill is swimming like a fish; a fish is drilling with a bent drill!

Select one and *see* it.

Benadryl to *typewriter*. A bent drill is using a typewriter; a typewriter is so durable that when you attempt to drill through it you bend a drill; you're typing on a bent drill.

See the picture you've selected.

Get ready to impress and amaze yourself.

Think of the first item: *pen*. If you formed a reminder-connection, a silly picture or association, between pen and something else—that something else should pop right into your mind. Pen forces you to see, reminds you of— *shoe*.

Shoe will immediately remind you of—book.

Now, think of book—and see if you can mentally hop-skip-jump right down to the end.

And you thought you had a poor memory!

> **There is no such thing as a poor memory! There are only trained and untrained memories.**

Try something else: Think of *typewriter*. If you're going backward, that should remind you of—bent drill—*Benadryl*.

Benadryl will immediately remind you of—fish.

Continue on your own. You'll hop-skip-jump up to the first item on the list!

I selected the eight items arbitrarily—they could represent anything.

If the eight "things" are being used to help you remember the *sequence* of a sales talk or speech, you'd say what you want to say about *pens*; that would lead you to your thoughts on *shoes*; then *books*—and on to the end of your talk.

And you didn't need notes!

If the eight "things" are being used to remind you of errands or appointments, you'd go see the man about the shipment (let's assume) of the ten gross of fountain *pens*; you'd go pick up your *shoes*; you'd buy the *book* you've been promising to get for a friend, and so on—until you pick up your repaired *typewriter*.

The Link System (so titled because you "link" one item to the next) is used to help with the three "R's" of memory: Register (in the first place), Remember, and Recall.

Link the items you need at the supermarket. Lists on pieces of paper (which you can lose or forget to take with you) are no longer necessary. And, when you have to go to the market again, form another Link—the one you formed yesterday served its purpose, has faded, and will not confuse the issue.

If you can Link eight "things," you can Link eighteen or twenty-eight. It makes no difference. Except that it will take longer to Link twenty-eight than eight. It would have, and always has, taken longer to remember twenty-eight things than eight things, whether or not a system is applied.

Try this list of things on your own, just to lock in the fact that the system works—beautifully!

Apple, lamp, scissors, cigarette, shoe
(just to show you that this won't become confused
with the Link you have already done),
nail, shirt, stamp, car, cup.

Show off a bit! Ask a friend to give you a list, and memorize it.

MEMORY BREAK #4

Two more of those pairs to learn:

Let 7 = K, hard c, hard g. (You can form a capital K with two mirror-image sevens on their sides.)

Let 8 = f, v, ph. Remember, we're interested in the *sound* the letters make. *Ph* makes the f sound. If you put a small tail at the center of an 8, it looks a bit like a handwritten small f.

1 = T,D	5 = L
T,D = 1	L = 5
2 = n	6 = J, sh, ch, soft g
n = 2	J, sh, ch, soft g = 6
3 = m	7 = K, hard c, hard g
m = 3	K, hard c, hard g = 7
4 = R	8 = f, v, ph
R = 4	f, v, ph = 8

Be sure you know these before you continue.

Speeches

I've seen lists of the ten things people fear most. Do you know what's number one on those fear lists? No, it's not death. It's the fear of getting up in front of people to deliver a speech!

What the lists don't show is that it's the thought of *forgetting* what you want to say that creates the fear in the first place.

Since a speech is a *sequence of thoughts*, the Link System is the technique to apply.

First, *extract* key words from your speech or talk. A key word is a word or phrase that *brings the entire thought to mind*, reminds you of that thought. Try it once, and you'll see that it's a simple thing to do. Read over your speech (which you wrote, so the assumption is that you know what you want to say) and underline a word or phrase that will remind you of each particular thought.

Then—*Link* those underlined key words. That's all. Because the best way to deliver a speech is thought for thought, not word for word, the Link of key words is really all you need.

The speech excerpt on the following page was delivered at a PTA meeting. Read it over once and you'll see that a Link of the four words in the left margin would remind you of that entire speech.

Ladies and Gentleman

I'm sure you're already aware of the problems that exist at this school. Certainly you're aware of the crowded conditions of the classrooms; a situation that has existed for some time now.

CROWDED

Some classrooms are handling twice as many students as they were originally built to handle. Busing children to other schools hasn't relieved the situation because the same number are being bused here. The problem remains unsolved.

Have you taken a close look at some of the seats and desks used by our children—when they're lucky enough to have them? In a recent survey, just about every third seat and every third desk proved to be in extremely poor condition and should be replaced. We've received many estimates for repairing or replacing all seats and desks where necessary, but so far no action has been taken.

FURNITURE

SALARIES

We have fine teachers, but I'll be surprised if they stay with us. You know that their salaries are low. All of them have to moonlight, and almost all are thinking of changing careers. Aside from ourselves, the parents, our teachers are the most important people involved in the upbringing and teaching of our children. At times, they are more important than we are. And yet they earn less than the man who takes care of your car, your teeth, your hair, your insurance, your clothes, or your plumbing! This situation must be remedied if we value the welfare and well-being of our children.

FIRE

Did your child tell you about the fire-drill fiasco of last week? Did he or she tell you that one of the alarms did not sound and that many teachers and children were not aware that a drill was in progress? Have you heard that one exit door was stuck and wouldn't open? Many children had to be led to another exit, which was being used by others. Had there really been a fire—you can imagine what the tragedy would have been.

And so on.

Apply the Same Technique for Remembering Scripts

I have a framed letter on my office wall from Academy Award-winning actress Anne Bancroft. She writes, in part:

> My most recent play would not have opened had not your systems made it possible for me to memorize an almost impossible-to-memorize script. Not only did it make an impossible task possible, but it made what is a usual drudgery part of the creative art.
>
> I would never have believed that memorizing lines could be as exciting, stimulating, and as much fun as acting itself! You are a Miracle Worker.

Thought for thought is the best way to think of delivering a speech; not word for word. But word for word is necessary for a script.

Apply the same system for a script as for a speech. Lock in the main thoughts by Linking key words. Remember the *main* thoughts, and the incidentals—the ifs, ands, and buts—will fall into place by themselves. For word-for-word memorization, go over the material more often. That's all.

Review the script. Go over it mentally again and again. It's about the only time I suggest using repetition.

Yes, it will take longer to memorize word for word than thought for thought—just as it would if you weren't applying my systems! Either way—thought for thought or word for word—will take much less time when you *do* apply the systems.

The same basic idea is used for remembering jokes and anecdotes. Link key words from the punch lines.

Our thoughts are so fleeting, no device for trapping them should be overlooked.
—Henry Hazlitt

Any Information Can Be Linked

No matter how esoteric the information. How would you go about learning the dynasties of China—Prehistoric China, Chou Dynasty, Ch'in Dynasty, Han Dynasty, Tang Dynasty, Ming Dynasty?

Start your Link with a "heading" picture, perhaps "Dinah's tea" or Chinese tea. To that, associate—a *prehistoric* animal (perhaps drinking Dinah's tea); the animal turns into a *chow* (or waits on a *chow* line); a chow bites your *chin*; a chin (with whiskers) is growing on your *hand*; a gigantic hand crawls out of a *tank* (or says "thanks"); there's a *mink* in the tank.

What About Retentiveness?

This is a question I'm usually asked at this point. If you've applied the ideas for a while, you know the answer. Lists of things that you want to remember for only a short time (a shopping list) will stay with you only *as long as you need them*.

The sequential (Linked) information you use over and over again *will become knowledge* in a short time. You'll know it. It's the use that controls retention.

If the list is something you use rarely, just review it— mentally—from time to time. You'll have the information when you need it.

All this holds true for whichever system or technique you learn in this book.

MEMORY BREAK #5

Let's mentally review the eight "pairs" I've taught you. Do that now. Then add the last two pairs to your "program."

Let 9 = P, B.   Two different letters, but they make the same consonant sound. The memory-aid: A 9 and a P are almost mirror images; a 9 is an upside-down *b*.

Let 0 = Z, S, soft c.   (That's zero, not ten.) Think of this for a second: the first sound in the word "zero" is "z"; the first sound in the word "cipher" is a soft c.

Now mentally review all ten "pairs" (that's all there are).

The Business Edge

In an article I wrote for the magazine *Nation's Business*, I spoke of the personal poll I'd conducted among a few thousand presidents and chairmen of the board of large corporations. The pertinent question was: How important is a good memory in your business? The four choices were: Not important; Important; Very important; and Essential.

Over 90 percent checked "Essential."

When the chairman of the board of a large, nationwide supermarket corporation introduced me as the keynote speaker at their annual meeting, he stated in no uncertain terms that he attributed his own rise mainly to his prodigious memory! Sure, he knew the business, but others knew it as well. In his words, his "edge" was his memory. Others in the company agreed. Through the years, this was the person everyone went to when a problem that had anything to do with remembering any information or specifics had to be solved.

I heard about people like that all the time. There's often that one person, in any position in a company, whom everyone seeks out for pertinent information. You'll hear "Oh, if you need a name or a place, a price, style number, phone number, address, see so-and-so; he (or she) will know." That's the person who has that extra "edge," the one who is ripe for spurting ahead, for being promoted to a more responsible position. That's the person who is noticed. And that's the key, being *noticed*. Noticed means not being overlooked. From show business, to clerking, to blue collar, to white collar, to junior executive, to executive, it's being noticed that makes the difference, that gives you that extra edge.

Those who learn and use my systems don't acquire "good" memories. The simple application of the systems, methods, techniques, will give you an *extraordinary* memory.

Most business and professional people are on the same raft, sailing the same rough seas. We live in what's been called the era of the "information explosion." It's been said that if all the new technological information surfacing each year were typed, double-spaced, on 8½ × 11 sheets of paper, those sheets, laid end to end, would encircle the earth. Somebody has to remember that information. *You* have to remember some of it.

One of the reasons you can't maintain the work load that you know you should maintain (even if you give up lunch hours and take work home) is the loss of time caused by a poor or an inefficient memory—a memory that isn't *working for you* at peak level. And I don't have to tell you that in business, time is money. Wasted time caused by an inefficient memory can easily cut into your profit margin.

The nitty-gritty: It is your capacity to retain and utilize knowledge that controls your business or professional life—and therefore your life-style. Learning and applying the systems taught in this book will enlarge your capacity to *learn*. And I believe that your capacity and desire to learn will regulate your life's work and your capacity to *earn*.

Applying my systems doubles the amount of work you can get out every day. It eliminates in advance careless errors, absentmindedness, doing the same job twice, and making mistakes because you didn't remember all the facts.

I'm aware that each business and professional person feels that his or her memory problems are unique. And they well may be. But let me assure you that it doesn't matter! After you learn the basics of the systems you'll see that using one idea in conjunction with another, twisting or manipulating them as needed, can help to solve and overcome *any* memory problem you may ever confront.

You'll be able to absorb the myriad business reports, technical material, and so on that consume so much time in half the time it takes you now.

There is also the sense of authority and confidence that a reliable memory gives you when you're discussing your product line with a business prospect or associate. Nothing sells better than facts, and when you have every fact at your fingertips, you are an authority.

Telephone numbers, lists, prices, style and model numbers, insurance policy numbers, stock quotations, business reports, new information, medical data, legal data, data of any kind—can be remembered easily and at will.

You can remember the name of every customer or client you meet. Most products today are pretty much the same as the competition's. The extra selling point is: *you*; the impression *you* make. And nothing impresses as much as being remembered.

A quick and reliable memory is an essential business tool.

From *The Guiness Book of World Records*

The lowest limit in enumeration among primitive peoples is among the Yancos, an Amazon tribe who can't count beyond *poettarrarorincoaroac*, which is their word for "three."

Imagine the memory problem that would arise if they could count to ten!

The Two Major "Difficult" Areas

Unfortunately, two of the most difficult areas of memory are also two of the most *important*. One area is conglomeration-of-sound—unfamiliar words, names of people, places, and things. It's a difficult area because we're dealing with abstracts, things that ordinarily cannot be visualized.

But the Substitute Word System solves that problem. It enables you to turn a conglomeration of sound into something meaningful—into a "thing" that *can* be visualized.

The other difficult (and important) area is *numbers*. Numbers are concepts: What "6" means to me and you is a thing that's 1 lower than 7 and 1 higher than 5. Ordinarily there's no way to visualize numbers.

Numbers

We've moved from the horse and buggy to supersonic flight in a short time. Why not make the same progress, the same strides, in the area of memory? Those strides have been made. I'll teach you the "supersonic" way to remember numbers—*any* numbers, alone or in conjunction with anything else.

Before I get to the concrete and definite system, I want to discuss a simple, general, and helpful idea that will show you how to keep, say, a 5- or 6-digit number in your mind for a short period of time. It's really just a way of *talking to yourself*! (That's what thinking really is, when you get right down to it.)

Assume that you see the number 96538 and then you have to turn to your typewriter and type it. What you'd usually do is to say mentally, "nine, six, five, three, eight." But by the time you've turned to your typewriter those numbers are a jumble; you've forgotten one or two digits, or their proper sequence.

Your confusion results from the way you say (think) those digits to yourself. You'll save yourself many turns to and from the typewriter this way: *Don't* think "nine, six, five, three, eight." Think "ninety-six, five thirty-eight." That's all. It'll stay with you, correctly, until you've typed it. Why? Instead of "thinking" five separate entities (nine, six, five, three, eight), you're thinking *two* entities (ninety-six and five thirty-eight). Also, it's a more *fluent*, rhythmic, thought—easier to repeat mentally.

‖ 73 ‖

Try it again: *24173*.

Don't think "two, four, one, seven, three," think "twenty-four, one seventy-three." Isn't it much easier?

Same idea if the number contains a zero. For 08294 think, "oh eight, two ninety-four." For 36048 think "thirty-six, oh forty-eight." If there's a double digit, *say* it—for 66461 think, "double six, four sixty-one."

If a number ends with 25 or 50 try this: Assume the number is 71325. Think "seven thirteen and a *quarter*" or "seven thirteen and a *half*" (71350), as if "thinking" money.

For a 6-digit number: 947142; think "nine forty-seven, one forty-two." It's simply easier to "transport" 6-digit numbers this way.

Handle an 8-digit number in similar fashion. Try 28194573: Think "twenty-eight nineteen, forty-five seventy-three."

But—I've caused more eyes to widen with surprise and pleasure, and gotten more gasps from people when they realize what they can do using the really simple, almost obvious, system for numbers I'm about to teach you.

THE "BREAKS" PAY OFF

> There is no better way to
> remember numbers than
> what I'm about to teach you.

Learn the system I'll teach you here, and you'll remember numbers of any kind easily, quickly, and efficiently—with fun, imagination, creativity, and *retention.*

For twenty-five years now at most of my seminars for business groups, I've shown a blackboard with two sequences like these on it:

01472711581463909212
A STARK NAKED WEIGHTLIFTER JUMPS
UP AND DOWN

Look at the two sequences for a moment.

After I've erased the blackboard, I ask, "How many remember the long number?" That usually gets a "you-gotta-be-kidding" kind of laugh. Then, "How many know the sentence?" And more than half the group calls out, "A stark naked weightlifter jumps up and down!"

The point! Simply this: At this moment, if you know the sentence (and it's easy to visualize a stark naked weightlifter jumping up and down) *you also know that 21-digit number!*

"What!?" Yes, of course you do. Remember those ten "pairs" you learned? Those pairs make up what I call the *Phonetic Alphabet*. I'll get a bit more specific about it in a moment, but right now let's look at it.

1 = T, D	6 = J, sh, ch, soft g
2 = n	7 = K, hard c, hard g
3 = m	8 = f, v, ph
4 = R	9 = P, B
5 = L	0 = z, s, soft c

Now, look at this:

A
stark   0147 (s,t,r,k)
naked   271 (n,k,d)
weightlifter   15814 (t,l,f,t,r)
jumps   6390 (j,m,p,s)
up   9 (p)
and   21 (n,d)
down   12 (d,n)

A s t a r k   n a k e d   w e i g h t l i f t e r   j u m p s
   0 1 47 2 7 1   15 81 4 6 3 9 0

u p a n d d o w n
  9   2 1 1   2

I could have used:

A one-legged hippopotamus swims
  2   5 7   1   9   9 1 3 0 0   3 0

from shore to shore
84 3 6   4 1 6   4

Or:

a pretty girl is like a melody
 9 4 1   7 45 0 5 7   3 5 1

Or:

Mary, Mary, quite contrary,
3 4   3 4   7 1 7 214 4

how does your garden grow
  1   0   4 7 41 2 74

Or any familiar or easily visualized phrase or sentence.

The Phonetic Alphabet

It would be silly, if not impossible, to try to find a familiar phrase or sentence to cover any series of numbers.

But that is *not* how the system works. I've used these phrases only to show you that if you know the Phonetic Alphabet, familiar, concrete, easy-to-visualize things will *tell you* the number you want to remember.

You've learned a few other things about the Phonetic Alphabet by looking at the phrases and their "number transpositions."

You've learned that vowels (a,e,i,o,u) have no number value. Neither do the letters w,h,y (they do not form consonant sounds).

A double letter represents *one* digit because it makes *one* sound. Look at "hippopotamus." That transposes to 9 (the double P makes *one* sound), then another 9,1,3,0. "Bellow" transposes to 95, not 955.

Silent letters are ignored. Knee = 2, not 72; knife = 28, not 728. The K is silent. Bomb = 93, not 939; the second b is silent.

Q makes the "k" sound, so it's 7. X transposes according to how it's pronounced in a word. In "anxious" the x is pronounced "k, sh" so it transposes to 76.

It's the *sound*, not the letter itself, that we're interested in. That's all you have to know.

I Cannot Visualize 14741

Neither can most people. But I can visualize myself taking a *truck ride*. To me—and shortly, to you—"truck ride" *means* 14741! Visualizing a truck ride is *the same as* visualizing 14741.

Because: T = 1, R = 4, K (ck—one sound) = 7, R = 4, D = 1.

$$\begin{array}{cccccc} \text{T} & \text{R U C K} & \text{R} & \text{I} & \text{D} & \text{E} \\ 1 & 4 & 7 & 4 & 1 \end{array}$$

Dark route, track rat, the (consider *th* the same as T or 1) rack red, tire crude, tar crud, and so forth, would all transpose to 14741. So would the one word, *triggered*.

The word *attention* transposes to 1262. The double t makes one sound, the "t" sound for 1. Then the "n" sound for 2. The next t does *not* make a "t" sound; in this word it makes a "sh" sound—that's 6. And then the final n for 2.

Can you come up with a word or phrase for 3475?

For 3475 you need these sounds, *in this order*: M,R,K,L.
Form the sounds in your mind.

Miracle is fine. Or, mare kill—more coal— mere gal—
my rack low—mower coil— murky law—mark well.

What word or phrase would fit each of the following
with our Phonetic Alphabet?

957—
91421—
0014—
2750—
62154—
941—
721—
821292—
1—
994—

957—black, pluck, buy lake
91421—butternut, better not, bitter nut
0014—sister, size tire, cyst raw
2750—necklace, nickels, neck less, no class
62154—chandelier, giant lure, giant liar
941—bread, brat, broad, poured, bright, beard
721—can't, count, gaunt, candy
821292—fountain pen, found no bone, fine tin pan,
    phoned in bin.
1—tie, die, dye, eat, hat
994—paper, pauper, beeper, baby hair, piper

Now that you know the ten "pairs," you only have to say mentally those sounds the numbers represent. You'll almost automatically form words or phrases. The vowels act as "wild" sounds; they can be used anywhere to help form words since they don't represent numbers.

When I was a young boy I once gave a candy store proprietress a five-dollar bill to pay for a 25-cent purchase. She gave me change for *one* dollar. When I shyly complained she said, "You gave me a dollar—now get out of here." I'm a "depression kid," and that money represented many months of saving pennies. I never forgot it. For years now, when I give out a twenty-dollar bill or larger I automatically glance at and remember its serial number, or at least the last four digits! (I make up a Phonetic Alphabet phrase, quickly.)

In two decades, it has paid off once. A coffee-shop cashier gave me change of a five-dollar bill. I said, "I gave you a twenty-dollar bill." She said, "No, you gave me a five-dollar bill." "Check the uppermost twenty-dollar bill in your cash register, and you'll see that its serial number is . . ." I said, rattling off the eight digits—and two letters. Without a word, the cashier handed me another fifteen dollars!

Now Let's Get to the Nitty-Gritty

You can remember this 12-digit number—522641639527—
in *seconds* by applying *two* of the techniques I've taught
you. The first, of course, is the Phonetic Alphabet.

522	641	639	527
linen	shirt	jump	link

These four words can be *pictured* and *can only* rep-
resent, or transpose to, their respective number groups.
But how will you remember the words themselves?
Simple. Apply the *Link System of Memory!*
Associate *linen* to *shirt*. Easy. Visualize a shirt made
of linen. Shirt to *jump*—see a shirt jumping. Jump to a
(chain) *link*. See chain links jumping.
Or—Link *linen* to *shirt* to *jumble* to *neck*.
You've remembered that number! And you also know
it backward. Try it.

Look at this number: 195471952127
If you thought of

table rocket balloon tank
1 95   4   7   1 9   5   2 1 2 7

and Linked those four things, you remembered that number in *seconds*.

If you were more familiar with the Phonetic Alphabet you could have shortened your Link to only three "things."

table   rocket   planting
1 95   4 7 1   9 5 21 2 7

A *table* is being launched like a *rocket*; a rocket is *planting* things. That's all!

You'll eventually fall into *standard transpositions*, which will save you time. For example, whenever I see 27, I use an *"ing"* ending: 952127—planting. (When I see an 0, I use a *plural*: 4710—*rockets*.)

How would you handle this number? (I'm breaking it into equal groups of three for teaching purposes.)

994   614   757   954

	994	614	757	954
	paper	ashtray	clock	bowler

Link *paper* to *ashtray*; ashtray to *clock*; clock to *bowler*. Perhaps: An ashtray is made of paper; you're using an expensive, antique clock for an ashtray; a gigantic clock is bowling—it's a bowler.

Try this one. Again, the number is broken into groups of four for teaching purposes. As you become proficient, you'll use the first words or phrases that come to mind, absorbing *any* number of digits.

4210   9483   5214   6127   9071

Come up with your own words or phrases before you look at the next page. (I've purposely included options for plural and "ing.")

4210	9483	5214	6127	9071
rents	perfume	launder	cheating	basket
runts	brief me	lender	shutting	biscuit
rants		lint raw	chatting	pass cat
		lander	shouting	pussy cat
		loan door		

If you Link *rents* to *perfume* to *launder* to *cheating* to *basket*—you've memorized, learned, this 20-digit number.

Of course, you rarely have to remember *just* a number; it would usually be remembered in conjunction with something else.

For example, if the above was your driver's license number, you'd *start* your Link with your picture of "driver" and Link driver to rents, to perfume, and so on. Then, you'd have the *two* pieces of information you need—the number, and what that number represents.

If you still remember the eight items in the first example Link on page 51 (the list that began with *pen*), you also know this number: 9269749527500869214519414! And if you memorized the list of ten "things" I gave you for practice (starting with *apple*), you also know a 27-digit number—forward and backward.

Telephone Numbers

If Mr. Cohen's telephone number is 981-9205, you'd *see*, perhaps, an ice-cream *cone* being b̲uffe̲d̲; a p̲enci̲l being buffed. Ice-cream cone reminds you of the person; buffed pencil tells you the number!

Mr. Bridges' telephone number is 951-4810. A *bridge* is being flown by a p̲il̲ot̲ (951); the pilot falls among ra̲ft̲s̲ (4810).

I usually break down a 7-digit telephone number into a word or phrase for the first three digits, and another word or phrase for the remaining four digits. But there's no rule that says you must do it that way.

If Ms. Carpenter's telephone number is 971-2101, you can associate a *carpenter* to b̲ig d̲enti̲st̲. (Or to ba̲ke̲d n̲o t̲oa̲st̲.)

You can make up standards for area codes and work them into your associations for out-of-town numbers. For New York City (212) you can use In̲dian̲ or an̲tenn̲a̲; associate either to "man hat." For 203, n̲o s̲eam̲ or n̲o s̲um̲ to "connect the cut" (Connecticut); associate n̲o t̲im̲e (213) to "lost angels" (Los Angeles); mu̲tto̲n̲ (312) to "chick car go" (Chicago); c̲asin̲o (702) to "gambling" or "never there" (Nevada); and so on.

Prices

Remember prices exactly the same way. Associate the item to the word or phrase that represents the price:

Toaster—$49.95 (toaster to rope pull)
Chair—$147.10 (chair to trick toes, or targets)
Radio—$27.50 (radio to necklace)
Pen—$19.75 (pen to topical, or tape coal)
Car—$8,409.00 (car to freeze up; fires up)

Don't worry about the decimal points—you'd *know*, for example that the radio you're pricing isn't selling for $2,750.00! If you do feel you need a reminder of decimal point placement, however, visualize someone or something *pointing* at the appropriate time in the association. Example: A neck is pointing at lace: $27.50. Or see something with a point, perhaps a knife, at the appropriate time. Your associations can be as specific as you want them to be.

Try it. Make the five simple associations; see how easy it is to remember the items and their prices. Sure, a bit of conscious effort is necessary. That's what makes it work—you're using your mind. And the more you use the systems you're learning here, the more effortless and automatic they become.

There is no limit to how many items and prices you can remember when applying the system.

As a matter of fact, it's when there are many that the system shines—it's more helpful than for just a few.

Better Business

Apply the Phonetic Alphabet to any area of work, business, study—or play—that entails remembering numbers. Say, for example, that you work in a retail clothing store where you have to remember style numbers of clothing items. All you have to do is make up a word or phrase that tells you the number and associate it to the item. If there are letters (of the alphabet) in the style number, you can "program" that in, too. You'll learn how later. One of my students remembered not only the style numbers for hundreds of items, but also the store number for fifty different stores in fifty different cities owned by his company. He told me he got a promotion and substantial raise because of this ability.

Another of my students, a race caller at Yonkers Raceway, used the system to associate horses' names to their post positions for each race. This enabled him to keep his eyes trained on the race, instead of glancing at a piece of paper each time he had to announce a horse's name.

And in the scholastic area, another of my students was almost expelled from law school because he did *too well* on an important test. He cited so many case numbers, precedents, page numbers, and so forth, that his professor thought he had to be cheating.

So many people have written to tell me they're enjoying their work more since applying the systems. One of the reasons for that enjoyment is that suddenly they're being noticed, and peers are asking them for information.

In business you need not only the hide of an elephant, but the memory of an elephant!

The
Peg
System

Screw a short *peg* into a wall—and you can hang your jacket or coat on it. Keep a *peg* in your mind—and you can hang any *thought* on it.

Earlier, you memorized eight items in sequence using the Link System. After doing that, if I'd asked you to tell me, say, the fourth item immediately, you couldn't do it without going over the Link and mentally counting or counting on your fingers to the fourth item.

There's another way, an easier method. Look at these ten words:

1. tie	6. shoe
2. Noah	7. cow
3. Ma	8. ivy
4. rye	9. bee
5. law	10. toes

Does something about each word seem familiar?

Familiarity Breeds

Each word, or *peg*, contains *only* the consonant sound that represents the vital number.

Within this context, the word *tie* can only represent the number 1—because it contains only the consonant "t" sound which, as you know, represents 1. Picture a necktie.

The word or name *Noah* contains only the (consonant) "n" sound; the "n" sound is 2. You can picture Noah's ark or the flood for this. (I simply picture a long gray beard, because Noah was an old man.)

Ma: Contains only the consonant sound "m" for 3. Picture your mother.

Rye: The "r" sound is 4. Picture a bottle of rye whiskey.

Law: "L" is 5. Picture a policeman, a judge, or a judge's gavel—anything that represents law.

Shoe: "Sh" is 6; shoe can represent *only* 6.

Cow: Hard "c" is 7.

Ivy: Contains only the consonant sound "v" for 8. Picture the ivy that clings to building walls.

Bee: "B" is 9.

Toes: "T" is 1; "s" is 0. *Toes* represents only 10 because the t and the s sounds are in that order. The same sounds in the word *suit* would represent, or transpose to, 01.

Ordinarily, remembering ten words by number like this would be strictly a rote operaton. But not now. I'm interested in *eliminating* rote memory, not in finding uses for it.

Look at the ten words once or twice. Because you already know the sounds of the Phonetic Alphabet, remembering them is a snap.

1. tie	6. shoe
2. Noah	7. cow
3. Ma	8. ivy
4. law	9. bee
5. rye	10. toes

ERROR!   ERROR!   ERROR!

Sorry, just wanted to make sure you were paying attention! I purposely made a couple of errors which you should have spotted immediately: 4 can't be *law* because 4 is "r"; 5 can't be *rye* because 5 is "L." Make sure you've got it straight.

If you know the words from 1 to 10, you also know them from 10 to 1—and in any order! Try it; test yourself.

These ten *Peg Words* have been arbitrarily selected. Other words would fit as well. There are only two criteria—the word must contain only the consonant sound(s) representing the vital number(s), and the word must be an easy-to-visualize (and therefore easy-to-associate) "thing."

I suggest you learn the words I use, which are those I've given you here. You'll have ten permanent Pegs in your mind upon which to hang anything, and you'll be able to use the same Pegs over and over again.

The memory is a treasurer to whom we must give funds, if we are to draw the assistance we need.
—Nicholas Rowe

Let's Learn Some New Information Now

Now you're ready to program your mind the way you would program a computer. We'll assume that you have to remember ten "things" by number, arising in random order.

For example, you want to remember (for whatever reason) that #6 is *checkbook*. Think about this for a moment.... Ordinarily, you could visualize (think of) checkbook because that's a tangible thing. But how in the world would you connect that to 6?

The problem no longer exists!

You now have a *Peg* for 6; a thing that represents or *means* 6 and, most important, a thing that can be visualized.

All you have to do is remind-connect your Peg Word for 6, *shoe*, to (in this case) *checkbook* as you've already learned to do!

Make that silly association—you're wearing checkbooks instead of shoes, or a shoe is writing a check, or you're writing a check on your shoe, or a large check is wearing shoes. Or select one you thought of yourself. *See* the picture.

This system can be invaluable for students or business people who must remember numbered material, like the Amendments to the Constitution, or computer codes, or the Ten Commandments, or a particular page number in a publication.

For #2, you want to remember *balloon*. Associate balloon to your Peg Word for 2, *Noah*. I see a long beard for Noah, so I'd visualize an old man with a large balloon instead of a beard. Select any picture you like, and *see* it for a second.

#9: *Lamp*. Associate *bee* to lamp. Perhaps millions of (lighted) lamps buzz around you like bees; or you switch on your lamp and millions of bees fly out, and so forth. *See* the picture you select.

#4: *Frying pan*. Form a reminder-connection between *rye* and frying pan—you want each to remind you of the other. You might see yourself drinking rye whiskey from a frying pan or a frying pan drinking rye whiskey.

#7: *Argyle*. I've thrown this one in purposely. Argyle is not a tangible thing. But so what? You can use socks to remind you of argyle. If not, "ah guile" or "ah girl" is close enough to serve as the reminder. Associate the picture you choose to *cow*. A cow's udders are socks; socks are coming out of a cow's udders instead of milk; a cow looks sexy and you think "*ah*, what a *girl*"; a cow is a thief and you think "*ah*, what *guile*."

#10: *Scissors.* Associate *toes* to scissors. Your toes are scissors; there are scissors between your toes; you're cutting off your toes with scissors (ecch!). All you need is one picture. *See* it.

#5: *Flower.* Associate whatever you're using to represent *law* to flower. A judge is banging a gigantic flower instead of a gavel; policemen are growing in your garden like flowers. *See* the picture you select.

#3: *Coin.* Your *Ma's* picture is on a coin or you're tossing Ma up into the air like a coin (heads or tails?). *See* the picture.

#1: *Cigarette lighter.* You're wearing a gigantic cigarette lighter instead of a *tie*, or you're lighting—burning—your expensive tie with a cigarette lighter (not impossible, but certainly silly enough).

#8: *Wristwatch.* Millions of *watches* are growing on a wall instead of *ivy*; you're wearing ivy on your wrist instead of a watch. *See* it.

Have you tried to form all ten associations?

It will work much faster when you do it on your own, when the Peg Words become second nature, which they will. Don't worry too much about speed at the beginning.

Now...

Presto chango...

You're a computer!

At first, your mind will do a few mental calisthenics. Thinking of #1 will remind you of the *sound* for #1—T (or D). The sound will tell you that the Peg Word for #1 is *tie*. After using these Pegs for a short time, you'll automatically eliminate the intermediary thoughts; when you think *1*, you'll think *tie* at the *same time*.

Okay, let's "RUN" the program with your computer mind. Think of #1—your computer mind "returns" *tie*. What does tie remind you of? Of course—you had visualized the silly picture of yourself wearing a cigarette lighter instead of a tie. So you *know* that #1 is cigarette lighter.

Think of #2. The Peg Word is... *Noah*. To what did you associate ark or beard? *Balloon*, of course.

#3. Think of your Peg Word... *Ma*. That should remind you of *coin* almost immediately.

#4. *Rye*. I feel you're way ahead of me. You were drinking rye whiskey from a *frying pan*.

#5. *Law*. A judge's gavel, or a policeman, reminds you of... *flower*.

I know you can do it on your own, but for completion's sake,...

#6. *Shoe* (this is the first item I threw at you). Instead of shoes, you're wearing. *, checkbooks*.

#7. *Cow*. This is the one that ordinarily might have stumped you, but not now. Perhaps you "saw" yourself milking a cow and coming out of the udders instead of milk, were...socks which, in turn, reminded you of... *argyle*.

#8. *Ivy*. What was growing on a wall instead of ivy? Millions of... *wristwatches*.

#9. *Bee*. Millions of bees flew out when you turned on your... *lamp*.

#10. *Toes*. You were cutting off your toes with...(ecch again!) scissors.

Well, did you know all or most of these? If you made the associations, the reminder-connections, there's no doubt that you did.

But...

Except for the fact that the ten things were given to you in random order (out of normal sequence) and you put them into sequence, you haven't done anything very different from the eight-item Link you did many pages ago. You know these ten "things" in sequence, from 1 to 10.

Ah, but no . . . your computer mind can do much more! When you think 4, your computer mind also thinks of the Peg Word for 4—*rye*. And rye immediately tells you—*frying pan*!

Impressed? You should be. See if you know the "thing" for

#8	_____	#9	_____
#2	_____	#7	_____
#10	_____	#3	_____
#5	_____	#6	_____
#1	_____	#4	_____

Can You Count Backward from 10 to 1?

Thinking of your Peg Words as you count (which should be just about automatic now) will tell you the ten "things" backward.

And it works either way. If I asked you to tell me the position of . . . *wristwatch*, what would your computer mind answer? Number 8, of course. Because your "personal computer" thought *wristwatch*, wristwatch reminded it of *ivy*, ivy contains only the one consonant sound "v," and "v" is 8! Your mind did it much faster than I can write it.

At what position is the balloon?
the scissors?
checkbook?
coin?
argyle?
flower?
lamp?
cigarette lighter?
frying pan?

You've Done What a Computer Can Do!

The ten "items you memorized so well could have been any "things." Any ten things you wanted—or needed— to know *by number*.

It's important for you to realize that those ten Pegs are there forever now. And they can be used over and over again. All my systems are means to an end; the end is the forming of knowledge. The systems register the information for you in the first place, then as you use the information it becomes *knowledge* and the associations fade—you no longer need them. If the information is a one-time thing, you'll do or remember the "things" and the associations will quickly fade.

Think of the Peg Words as a child's magic slate. After the memorized information has been used or has become knowledge, the sheet of plastic is lifted, clearing the slate. Then the Peg Words are ready to be used again!

Here's another set of ten things. This is optional—you don't have to memorize these if you feel you definitely understand the idea. But it can't hurt!

When you're thoroughly familiar with the Peg Words, you won't have to do any of the "middle man" mental calisthenics. The entire process will work many times faster. But don't worry about that now. Just remember that an hour ago you couldn't have done what you've just done, and are about to do, at *any* speed.

Make these reminder-connections:

3	(Ma) to tree	6	(shoe) to playing cards
8	(ivy) to tennis racket	9	(bee) to apple
4	(rye) to attaché case	2	(Noah) to Mr. Cohen
1	(tie) to picture frame		(use cone)
10	(toes) to bulb	7	(cow) to marble
		5	(law) to book

After you've made the association for each, try some variations. Put the ten things in correct numerical order; see if you know them from 1 to 10. Then do it backward, out of numerical order, inside-out!

A question may be running through your mind: "But what if I want to remember *more* than ten things by number?"

Part of the beauty of the system is that it's *unlimited!* So long as you know the ten pairs of the Phonetic Alphabet, you can make up a Peg Word for any number. Even if the number is a "squintillion"—so long you have to "squint" to see all the zeros.

If you needed a word (really a picture) always to represent 74, think of the vital sounds "k—r." You'll almost automatically think *car.* And that *is* the Peg Word for 74. It can represent *only* 74; there are *no decisions to make.*

11	=	tot	16 =	dish
12	=	tin	17 =	dog
13	=	tomb	18 =	dove
14	=	tire	19 =	tub
15	=	towel	20 =	nose

Familiarize yourself with Peg Words 11 through 20, and you can memorize twenty things by number exactly as you did ten.

New knowledge is acquired by being connected to what we already know.

I'll list the Peg Words from 21 to 100 on the next page. Whether or not you want to learn these Peg Words is up to you. If you feel that you'll never need more than twenty Pegs, don't bother. You can always make them up if and when you need them, if you know the sounds of the Phonetic Alphabet.

It won't take you very long to learn them, anyway.

Some of the Peg Words are used for remembering weekly appointments, so you might want to familiarize yourself with them.

Simply go over them once or twice, select a picture you'll see for each word, and you'll become familiar with them.

21. net	41. rod	61. sheet	81. fit
22. nun	42. rain	62. chain	82. phone
23. name	43. ram	63. chum	83. foam
24. Nero	44. rower	64. cherry	84. fur
25. nail	45. roll	65. jail	85. file
26. notch	46. roach	66. choo-choo	86. fish
27. neck	47. rock	67. chalk	87. fog
28. knife	48. roof	68. chef	88. fife
29. knob	49. rope	69. ship	89. fob
30. mouse	50. lace	70. case	90. bus
31. mat	51. lot	71. cot	91. bat
32. moon	52. lion	72. coin	92. bone
33. mummy	53. loom	73. comb	93. bum
34. mower	54. lure	74. car	94. bear
35. mule	55. lily	75. coal	95. bell
36. match	56. leech	76. cage	96. beach
37. mug	57. log	77. coke	97. book
38. movie	58. lava	78. cave	98. puff
39. mop	59. lip	79. cob	99. pipe
40. rose	60. cheese	80. fuzz	100. disease; thesis; diocese

Link or Peg?

When you need to decide whether to apply the Link or the Peg System to solve a memory problem, it's a simple choice. If you want to remember things in sequence only, use the Link. If it would be better to remember the things by number, use the Peg.

The Substitute Word System is used with either—to help you make a word or thing meaningful that cannot otherwise be visualized.

A lieutenant colonel in the air force who had read one of my books was shot down over North Vietnam in 1966. He was put into solitary confinement—with no reading or writing material—until 1973. He told me (and the viewing audience of "To Tell the Truth") that he'd preserved his sanity during those seven years by mentally reviewing my systems—the Peg Words, Alphabet Words, and so on. He began to teach them to other prisoners via Morse code, tapping on his cell wall with a pebble. Others taught it to others; they memorized philosophy, poetry, thousands of foreign words, mathematics, biology, and names of all the other prisoners. The officer said that he just wanted to tell me "how much your work meant to all of us behind the bamboo wall."

Using the three main ingredients of the memory system, you can solve any memory problem. You've already brought your memory (for names and faces, foreign language vocabulary, lists of things in sequence or by number) up to an unprecedented level by utilizing what you've learned.

Now that you understand what the techniques can do, you should be able to solve any memory problem that comes up. What you have to do is slightly alter the techniques so that they fit and solve the particular memory problem. You have the knowledge: *Use* it. I've taught you what I feel are the important, vital, specific memory techniques.

The Systems Are Flexible.

I think it's important for me to show you just how flexible these systems can be. And that's what the following Bonus Application sections demonstrate: the variety of areas to which these systems can be applied—to help you at home, at school, at work—in ways that will impress others and help you get what you want.

A man's real possession
is his memory.
In nothing else is he rich,
in nothing else is he poor.
—*Alexander Smith*

BONUS APPLICATION:
APPOINTMENTS

You can remember the things you want to do during a day by Linking the appointment/errands or by Pegging them by number. Just review your Link or Peg every so often during the day.

For many this will suffice. But to show you how flexible and specific the ideas are, we'll delve a bit deeper into appointment/errands.

How would you like to always remember your
wife's birthday?
Easy.
Just forget it once!

Compartments Are All You Need

Each compartment will be the day/time slot, the thing you already know, to which you can reminder-connect the new thing.

You already have those compartments for single day/hour appointment/errands. Use your Peg Words from, say, 1 to 12, to encompass twelve hours. (Use 1 to 24 to encompass 24 hours.) If you want to remember your dental appointment at 9 o'clock, associate *bee* to dentist.

You have a 1 o'clock luncheon appointment with Mr. Randall—see a *doll run*ning (run doll; Randall) up and down your *tie*. And so on.

In the morning, or the night before, mentally go over your Peg Words. You might want to start with, say, 8— 8 o'clock in the morning. So you'd think—ivy, bee, toes, tot, tin, tie, Noah, Ma, rye, law, shoe, cow—which takes you to 7 o'clock in the evening. When you think of a Peg Word to which you've associated an appointment/errand, that appointment/errand will immediately come to mind. Go over your Peg Words periodically during the day.

Do it every day.

Weekly Appointment/Errand Compartments

Okay, how about all those next-week appointments you need to remember? Your compartments must represent a specific day *and* hour. The best way is to consider *Monday* the first day of the week, because it's normally the first business day of the week:

Let:

Monday = 1	Friday = 5
Tuesday = 2	Saturday = 6
Wednesday = 3	Sunday = 7
Thursday = 4	

Let the first consonant of the compartment word represent the day of the week and the next consonant represent the hour of the day.

Because Monday is the first day, each compartment word for a Monday appointment will begin with the T or D sound, representing 1. So in this context, the word *tot* can only represent Monday (1st day) at 1 o'clock.

tin—Monday at 2	dish—Monday at 6
tomb—Monday at 3	dog—Monday at 7
tire—Monday at 4	dove—Monday at 8
towel—Monday at 5	tub—Monday at 9

What about 10, 11, and 12 o'clock? Use "0" for 10; no confusion possible since there is no "zero" o'clock. So *toes* represents Monday at 10 o'clock. Make up a word, within the system, for 11 and 12 o'clock. For example, for Monday (1) at 11 o'clock, you could use d̲ated̲, tout̲ed̲, or tot̲ed̲. For 12 o'clock—titan̲, tighten̲, dead̲en̲.

Do you see the simplicity of the idea?

An appointment comes up for, say, next Monday at 4 o'clock. The compartment, or slot, is *tire* because that represents Monday at 4. Associate the appointment to *tire* just as you've already learned. Use whatever you have to use in the association.

For example, say you have an appointment at Growth Company at 412 9th Street with Mr. Brown. If all you need is the company name you might simply visualize a *growth* on a tire. If you want to be reminded of the address you might "see" that growth turning rotten (412) and moving up (9th St.). If you want to remember Mr. Brown, see the tire (with the rotten growth moving up) *drown*ing, Drown-Brown. (Or you could picture a brown tire— although *drown* is a stronger slap in the face.)

It takes much longer for me to write than for you to *do*.

Next Monday morning (or Sunday night) go over your compartments (Peg Words) for Monday. Each associated appointment/errand will pop into your mind!

You need only try it to be convinced.

What about daytime/nighttime hours?
What about appointments on the half hour?
Quarter hour?
Three quarter hour?

Don't create problems where none really exists. If you have an 11 o'clock dental appointment, you know that it's at 11 A.M., not 11 P.M. Common sense is all that's needed. You can, however, make the system work as specifically as you want it to. Include a word in your association to tell you the minutes. If your appointment with Mr. Brown at Growth Company is for 4:18, get a *dove* (18) into the picture.

I never bother with this because, for me, it ordinarily isn't necessary. I use only half hours. I include a *half grapefruit* in any association to tell me that it's on the *half* hour. If an appointment is at quarter past an hour, I use my on-the-hour compartment. If it's a quarter to the hour, I use the half hour *before*. I'm fifteen minutes early in those cases. In fact, true memory usually tells me the exact time; all I need is the reminder.

You can get a *quarter* (twenty-five-cent coin) into your association to represent a quarter past an hour, or a pie with a couple of slices missing (three-quarters of a pie) to represent 45 minutes past an hour, which, of course, is the same as a quarter to the next hour.

You can include anything in an association to remind you of whatever you like. Just make up a standard, and use it whenever you want to be reminded of that particular piece of information.

You can, for example, always include *poem* in your picture (one of the things in the picture is reciting a poem) to tell you that it's a P.M. appointment. If there's no poem in the association, then it's an A.M. appointment.

Or, use *aim* to represent A.M. One of the things in your picture is aiming a rifle.

It's up to you—use what's best for you.

The compartment words for Tuesday are the Peg Words starting with net (2nd day, 1st hour). Net, nun, name, Nero, nail, notch, neck, knife, knob, nose (N = 2nd day; S = 0 or 10 o'clock). For 11 o'clock: knitted, knotted, knighted. For 12 o'clock: Indian, antenna.

Wednesday: mat, (m = 3rd day: T = 1st hour), moon, mummy, mower, mule, match, mug, movie, mop, mouse. For 11 o'clock: mated, or imitate. For 12 o'clock: mitten, mutton, or maiden.

Thursday (4th day): rod, rain, ram, rower, roll, roach, rock, roof, rope, rose. For 11 o'clock: rotate or raided. For 12 o'clock: rotten, written, or rattan.

Friday (5th day): lot, lion, loom, lure, lily, leech, log, lava, lip, lace. For 11 o'clock: lighted or loaded. For 12 o'clock: laden or Aladdin.

Saturday (6th day): sheet, chain, chum, cherry, jail, choo-choo, chalk, chef, ship, cheese. For 11 o'clock: cheated or jaded. For 12 o'clock: jitney, chutney, or shut in.

Sunday (7th day): cot, coin, comb, car, coal, cage, coke, cave, cob, case. For 11 o'clock: cadet or coated. For 12 o'clock: kitten or cotton.

Once you've locked in that Monday is the first day of the week, Tuesday the second day, and so on, you will find using the compartment words simple and crystal clear. (You can, of course, change the system to make any day the first day.)

Any appointment/errand that comes up for next week is easily "filed" into its compartment by associating the appointment to the proper word—the word that can represent *only* that particular day/hour.

Each morning or night before, starting next Monday, go over your words for that day and you'll know what you have to do that day—and at which hour!

BONUS APPLICATION: PERPETUAL CALENDAR

If it would be a help to be able to figure out the day of the week for any date during a year without looking at a calendar, you may find this useful.

Memorize this number the way you've learned: 744163152742. (You might Link crier, touch me, talon, crown.)

This 12-digit number consists of the date of the *first Monday* of every month of the year 1985. (Use the appropriate numbers for whichever year you need; I'm using 1985 as the example.)

Knowing that number enables you to work out the day of the week for any date within that year.

One example: My birthday is May 4 (yes, I'm a Taurus). Knowing that the first Monday in May 1985 falls on the 6th of the month (look at the 5th digit in the 12-digit number; May is the 5th month) makes it a simple matter to calculate that the 4th of May falls on Saturday.

There are ways to use a particular 12-digit number all the time for every year, but the calculations become too complicated. It's easy enough to memorize the new 12-digit number at the beginning of each year.

BONUS APPLICATION: KNOW YOUR ABCs

There may be times when you'll have to remember letters of the alphabet. It's easy. Use these "alphabet words," each of which sounds enough like the letter it represents to bring it to mind effectively.

A — ape
B — bean*
C — sea
D — dean
E — eel
F — half; effort
G — jeans
H — ache; age
I — eye
J — jay (bird)
K — cake; cane
L — el (elevated train); elf, ell
M — emperor; hem

N — hen
O — oh!; eau (French for water); old
P — pea
Q — cue (stick)
R — hour (clock); art
S — ess-curve; ass
T — tea
U — ewe
V — veal; victory
W — Waterloo**
X — eggs; X-ray
Y — wine
Z — zebra

*Bee for B might confuse with the Peg Word for 9.
**For Waterloo, picture Napoleon.

Now you can visualize something that represents the squiggles that are each letter of the alphabet!

The alphabet words come in handy in many situations. For example, we discussed remembering style numbers. Some style numbers contain letters *and* numbers. Now you can include something in your association picture to *tell* you the letter by including the proper alphabet word.

The alphabet words will be useful if you have to remember a formula or equation or stock market symbols.

The license plate number 175-AQ-38 is easily remembered by associating (Linking) *tackle* to *ape* to *cue* to *movie*. (You won't be confused into thinking that *ape* and *cue* represent 97 because you *know* they're *alphabet* words.)

The letters of the alphabet have now become things you can visualize. You can manipulate them anyway you want. If you remind-connect your Peg Word to the proper alphabet word, you'll know the *numerical position* of every letter—if that's something you'd like to, or need to, know. (Tie to ape, Noah to bean, Ma to sea, rye to dean, law to eel, shoe to half, cow to jeans, ivy to ache, bee to eye, toes to jay [bird], tot to cake, and so on to notch to zebra.)

Do this and you'll also have a 26-word emergency Peg Word list!

BONUS APPLICATION: ABSENTMINDEDNESS

I'm sure you've heard of the absentminded professor who slammed her husband and kissed the door!

How many times have you opened your refrigerator door and stared into it only to wonder why you are there? How often do you drive yourself crazy trying to figure out where you left your keys, pen, or eyeglasses?

I devised the system for eliminating absentmindedness over thirty years ago for strictly selfish reasons—I wanted to get rid of my own time-wasting, aggravating absentmindedness. The first time I published the system was in 1957. In all the years since then, I've received more mail, calls, and comments about it than about any of my other ideas.

Perhaps that's because the system is so easy to apply. All you need is the knowledge of association, or reminder-connections, which you already have.

Accept This Fact

The word "absentminded" itself tells you what the problem is. You do certain actions while your mind is absent.

When a problem is easily and clearly seen, the solution, too, is usually easy and clear. In this case, just make sure that your mind is *present* at the moment you do those certain actions.

When you put something down without thinking about that action at that moment, you are not being *originally aware*. You are not registering that piece of information. You can't *forget* where you put that something, since you didn't *remember* where you put it in the first place.

You know the solution: *Think of the activity during the moment of that activity.* That means: Make sure your mind is present, not absent.

But how?

You already know that it's necessary to *force* your mind to pay attention. You also know that forming an association or reminder-connection is what forces that attention and pinpoints concentration. So get into the habit of forming a silly association—between the *item* and the *place*—whenever you "just put something down!"

One of the things that plagued me years ago was searching for a pencil that I'd perched behind my ear. I solved the problem easily when I started *seeing* that pencil going *into* my ear each time I put it *behind* my ear! I could almost feel the pain.

How did that help? Without breaking physical or mental stride I brought my mind to that activity during that fleeting moment. I forced my mind to take note of the activity *at that moment*. I *forced* original awareness.

Not in over thirty years have I ever again searched for the pencil that's behind my ear.

Nor do I ever search for my eyeglasses pushed up on my forehead, or that I "just put down" somewhere. I always associate eyeglasses to where I put them *when* I put them there. If I momentarily put them on a television set, I see the antenna going through, and shattering, the lenses. The next time I think of glasses (when I need them), my mind instantly responds *television set*!

Yes, you have to form the habit. Force yourself to do it the first few times and the habit is formed.

Although it takes no time, you may think it does and be hesitant about trying it. Well, think of the time it will *save* and you'll lose your hesitation.

Do you put away treasured items for safekeeping, then forget where you hid them? Make an association at the moment of hiding. You hide a treasured book under your shirts. See a shirt reading a book.

You think of ketchup, which you have to get out of a kitchen cupboard. The moment you think of it, see ketchup squirting all over you. I assure you, you won't stare into the cupboard wondering what you wanted and why you're there.

There's an old Gracie Allen joke:

When you put a roast in the oven, put a small roast into the oven at the same time.
When you smell the small one burning, you'll be reminded that the large one is ready!

It's funny because there's truth to it. But instead of burning an expensive roast, drop your potholder to the middle of your kitchen floor when you put the roast in the oven. That will be a constant reminder that you have a roast in the oven!

It's an old idea of the string-on-finger family. I've enlarged on the concept through the years.

If you think of something while you're in bed, half asleep, reach over and turn your clock away from you, or reach down and toss a slipper under your bed. Something out of place will jog your memory in the morning. As a matter of fact, I call them *memory joggers*.

Now, what about remembering to take home the book you bought during lunch hour?

Apply the Basic *Reminder* Principle

What's the last, or next-to-last, thing you do or see when leaving your office? Associate the book or whatever you want to remember—even if it's an activity like making a phone call—to that last thing you do.

Perhaps your last action is checking if your secretary's door is locked. Form a silly association between that door and book, or whatever. As a backup, you can also associate book to the elevator man, to whom you say "good night" each day. You've got two reminders.

When you leave your house for an evening out, see yourself switching on your telephone answering machine with your *head*, or locking your door by sticking your entire *foot* into the keyhole. You've *forced* your mind to be present during the actions.

You'll never again ruin an evening at the theater wondering whether you turned on the answering machine, locked the door, unplugged the iron, switched on the burglar alarm, or what-have-you!

BONUS APPLICATION: SPELLING

Most common spelling "misteaks" are habitual ones—there is a persistence of error.

All you have to do to correct these errors is to "program in" the correct spelling at persistent trouble spots.

Example: "Those lines are ALL parALLel."

As discussed at the beginning of this book, this is a good way to associate and correct spelling trouble spots. This one will help you to remember that the word "parallel" is spelled parALLel, not paralELL.

Visualize that sentence, and you've made something you already know (the spelling of "all") help you remember a new thing, the spelling of "parallel."

The same idea will work for many words.

It's neCESSary to clean a CESSpool.

Don't EAT lEATher.

I take a BUS to BUSiness.

HERE is wHERE I want to be.

There's no trAGEdy to AGE.

It's a FEAT to balance a FEATher.

My PET learned by rePETition.

It was the END of my friEND.

"All right" is the opposite of "all wrong." ("Alright" is incorrect.)

DeSSert comes after diNNer (double n reminds you of double s), or I want *doubles* of deSSert.

A deSert is full of Sand (single s).

It was a coLOSSal LOSS.

NavAl as in nAvy. NavEl as in bElly button.

We were WED on a WEDnesday.

Expen$e: See that dollar sign for S; it's not "expenCe."

A principLE is a ruLE.

The school princiPAL is my PAL.

FrancEs as in hEr or shE.

FrancIs as in hIm or hIs.

Try to apply these ideas to any word you've had trouble remembering how to spell correctly. Let your school-age children try to apply them. You'll see amazing results.

BONUS APPLICATION: STUDENT AID

> **There Is No Learning
> Without Memory!**

You can teach the ideas in this book to your school-age children (or any-age students). It's amazing how many different ways they'll be able to apply it to schoolwork.

There are three main steps to *learning*:

1. Searching for information.
2. Retaining that information.
3. Using that information.

Our schools help with 1 and 3. I'm giving you the help you need with 2!

In particular, in this book students should review the sections on remembering the meanings of English and/or foreign words, and the section on spelling. As they advance in grades, students will find the memory systems taught here invaluable in helping them succeed in school.

Early School Grades

Most of the information that young people have to "learn" (meaning "remember") is easily handled with the Link System or single, individual associations plus—always— the Substitute Word System. For children, this technique will turn studying into a game instead of a boring task.

Remembering states and capitals is a clear example. How easy it is to associate the capital city to the state. Make up a Substitute Word for the state and one for the capital city—associate one to the other. That's all.

Examples: A *boy see*ing (Boise) an *Idaho* potato; *Mary land*ing on *an apple* (Maryland-Annapolis); throwing *little rocks* at an *ark* (Arkansas); *Santa Claus* (Santa Fe) wearing a shiny *new Mexican* sombrero (New Mexico); a girl named Helen or *Helena* climbing a *mountain* (Montana); and so on.

A teacher friend of mine called excitedly one day to tell me that she taught her eight-year-old students to remember American Indian names in minutes and that the children enjoyed it tremendously.

She had them help her to think of Substitute Words or phrases and to help with the silly pictures. *Cherry key* (Cherokee), to *eye patch* (Apache), to *sue* (Sioux), to *shy Ann* (Cheyenne), to *never hoe* (Navaho), to *hawk* (Mohawk), to *Sammy in hole* (Seminole), to *here a coin* (Iroquois), to the National Anthem—"*Oh say* can you see"—(Osage—I love that one). Leave it to the children.

Make up a Substitute Word for each United States president and Link them. You'll know not only their names but the correct *sequence*. Washing or washing machine to Adams apple to "d'ja have a son?" (Jefferson) or chef and son to mad at son (Madison) to a man row or Marilyn (Monroe) to a dam (Adams) to jack (Jackson) to van or van bureau (Van Buren) to hairy son, and so on.

With the Phonetic Alphabet, it is quite simple to "lock" historical dates into students' memories. For example: "Napoleon's efforts were futile at Waterloo" will make it easy to remember that Napoleon was defeated at Waterloo in 1815. (Futile or fatal can represent only 815. You'd know that the date isn't 815 B.C. or 815 A.D., nor could it be 2815! So, 1815 is the critical date.) Neil Armstrong was the first man to step onto the moon. Picture him stepping into ketchup, and you'll be reminded that it happened in 7–69, July 1969.

Older students can associate dates to events, *sequences* of events, and so on, in any of their schoolwork. Bear in mind that these are aids to memory. It's important that you understand what's being taught first; then apply the systems.

Understanding is, itself, a memory aid to learning!

BONUS APPLICATION: READING, CONCENTRATION, AND LISTENING TECHNIQUES

Although the techniques that follow can be enormously helpful to students, they are *not only for students*.

To succeed in any area—at home or at work—we must all be able to gain as much as we can, as quickly as we can, from what we read and from what we hear.

Reading

One of the primary ways we absorb information and knowledge is, of course, through reading. The techniques taught in this book enable you to remember reading matter *as* you read.

Just about any fact you read can be *visualized*, made tangible, and then *associated*—names of people, places, things; numbers; letters; dates. I'm interested, as are most people, mainly in informational reading matter. But the systems are helpful even for pleasure reading.

In *War and Peace*, Tolstoy introduces characters with long Russian names and explains who the characters are related to and how they are related. Some are not mentioned again for many pages. If you're really interested in the continuity of the epic, you probably have to flip back and search to find out who that character is. That searching time would be saved if you originally make up a Substitute Word for the character's name and associate it to the Substitute Word for the "related" character— plus, if you like, a word that tells you the relationship.

What about nonfiction?

Since most informational reading is sequential, you'd use the Link system. My suggestion is to first read the material quickly to get the overall gist of it. Then, read it again, applying the systems and associating what you feel is important to remember. An example:

> Across the Mediterranean Sea from Egypt lies a rocky peninsula with an uneven coast—the mainland of Greece. East of the peninsula, in the Aegean Sea, are many islands, large and small. Here was the home of Greek civilization.
>
> The first Greeks probably came to the area about 2000 B.C. By 1500 B.C. some of them had a civilization. They wrote, they painted, and they built great palaces. But they spent most of the time fighting. About 1100 B.C., they were conquered by other Greek tribes who were not as civilized.

Start your Link with a "heading" picture—*grease*. Headings are important. In some cases, simply Linking *headings* will give you the vital information contained in an article or book. For this example, let's do a Link of the facts in the two paragraphs.

Follow Me:

There's lots of *grease* on a *cross*; a cross dives into the *sea* to *meditate* (across the Mediterranean Sea); the meditating cross swims away from a pyramid or Sphinx (Egypt) to a gigantic *pen* that's on an *uneven rock*. You could see the *pen* taking *insulin* (pen insulin–peninsula). The pen *coasts*—it has a *mane* and buckets of *grease land* on that mane.

Review: This partial Link reminds you that across the Mediterranean Sea from Egypt is a rocky peninsula with an uneven coast; the mainland of Greece.

Continue: Lots of *yeast* is on the pen which causes the pen to grow a beard—it's *aging*. (East of the peninsula, in the Aegean Sea.) This gigantic beard breaks up into *many large and small pieces* (islands). Lots of *grease* falls onto the pieces and lives there, building *homes* (home of Greek civilization). A large *nose* is being built. (Nose = 20. This is to remind you of 2000 B.C. You could use n̲oi̲s̲e̲s̲ sue or n̲i̲c̲e̲ s̲i̲s̲, if you'd rather.) A gigantic *towel* (15 for 1500 B.C.) covers the homes and the nose. People are *writing* and *painting* on the towel. One painting is of a *palace*; the writers and painters fight each other most of the time. An *uncivilized tot conquers* the fighters.

I've included all the facts, but when you try it on your own you'll find that one *key word or thought* will remind you of a few facts. You have to decide what to include in your Link. Think back to when you were studying for tests in school. You made instant decisions as you read. If you thought that a fact would be used on a test, you tried to remember it—if you didn't think it would be used, you didn't bother. You'll automatically be doing the same now, whether you're reading a law journal, medical article, or technical manual.

And even though you used a Link (a system used to remember things in sequence), you'll know the facts in any order. If you worked along with me and really made the pictures suggested on the preceding page, you'll see this is so. Test yourself.

Please understand this essential point: Although it will take you longer to read this way, you will be reading effectively and meaningfully. And, you'll more than make up the time because you won't have to go over the material again and again! After some practice, you'll be able to Link facts almost as quickly as you normally read.

Now I want to discuss not a specific memory system, but some ideas that you should be able to "merge" with the memory systems.

Reading well and effectively entails more than the simple concept of recognizing words. Passive, mechanical reading has to be changed to active, aggressive reading. Your reading will become active and aggressive only when you start trying to boil the torrent of words into thoughts. That's what effective reading is—the art of boiling down dozens, hundreds, and thousands of words into a few vital thoughts.

> **Effective reading is a search—a search for ideas, thoughts, answers.**

The first rule for effective reading is to *locate* main ideas, thoughts, and answers within the mass of words that contain them. I say "answers" because to concentrate on informational matter it's better to ask questions of yourself and of the material.

You must learn to get to the guts of reading material quickly, to separate the few really important thoughts from all the waste words and unnecessary details that surround them—separating the wheat from the chaff, as it were.

Locate, then separate or *spear* each thought, idea, and answer out of its surrounding, sometimes vague cacophony of words.

Boil each idea or thought down to a few easily remembered words. Three simple rules: locate, spear, and boil. Like a spear-carrying hunter searching for food who has to *locate* the prey, *spear* it, then *boil* it, you must locate the thought, spear it out of unnecessary detail, then boil it down to a few easily remembered (for you, now) words.

Applying the systems you've learned does the spearing and boiling down for you. You can start locating even before you actually start to read. Start by *pre-reading* the material. Glance over it before you start normal reading. A few moments spent on pre-reading can save hours. Check chapter and section headings, foreword, bold type, opening and closing paragraphs, index.

The point of pre-reading is to look for the answers to those questions you've asked yourself.

Concentration

If, after pre-reading, you decide that the material does answer questions, you have to read it with concentration.

Applying the *trained-memory systems* is the best way to force yourself to pinpoint your concentration. But here are a few other basic thoughts on concentrating while *reading* and *listening*.

Concentration is *exclusive attention* on one object or subject. How do you give your entire, exclusive attention to one subject? Apply the golden rule of concentration:

Get yourself involved!

Next problem: How do you get yourself involved?

Ask questions.

That starts you thinking.

When reading informational material, read to find specific answers to specific questions. Remember: Unless you're reading solely for enjoyment, reading is a search for information or for knowledge. You're looking for answers to questions.

Before you start to read, ask yourself exactly what you want the article, report, book, magazine, or newspaper to answer. List the questions if necessary, but *ask* those questions first.

Use the six "tiny keys to knowledge":

What, Why, Where, When, Who, and How.

Example: Assume you're about to read an article called "A Plan to Free Cuba." Some of your questions may be: *What* is the plan? *Who* is its author? *What* are his or her qualifications? *What* action does the plan require? *How* long would it take? *What* are its chances of success? *When* can it begin? And so on.

This self-questioning automatically involves you with the material. You're pinpointing your exclusive attention on important questions and preventing distraction by minor details! You're *involved*. Read with your questions in mind. Each sentence is judged on this basis: Does it or doesn't it answer one of your questions? If it doesn't, skim it, and continue to search for answers.

If a sentence does answer a question, slow down and read it carefully. Be sure you understand it, then *associate that answer to your question*. You may want to get more actively involved—pick up a pencil and *underline the key words* of that sentence or answer. Mark up the book or article. You can then *Link* the underlined key words.

If you underline only a few things you should feel good. Think of all the excess material—the padding—you've eliminated. A sentence that doesn't answer one of your questions is not worth your time.

To Wrap It Up: In order to involve yourself with and to concentrate on reading material: (1) Form questions; and (2) Read to find answers to those questions. Apply these simple techniques and you're learning how to turn reading material into a *personal acquisition*, how to work toward the *mastery* of the material.

Not only will you be concentrating and absorbing more than usual, but if you underline the answers you find, you're creating a list of key words you can Link in order to remember them.

When you start applying these ideas they may, and should, slow you down. Eventually, you'll see that you're saving time. You won't have to go over and over the same material. So don't worry about the time it takes.

Remember: How quickly you get through reading material is not as important as how much of the material gets through to you!

Are the same techniques applied to *listening*?
Yes; basically.

Listening

Apply the same techniques to gain information from what you hear. The bulk of the problem is learning to *maintain attention*. Again, if you try to Link facts that you hear you must, automatically, be forcing yourself to listen. That's the best way.

But, for your general knowledge...

You must focus your exclusive attention and maintain that attention. It is, unfortunately, easier to let your mind wander. You think about four times as fast as someone speaks. That large gap allows the intrusion of distracting thoughts that create mind-wandering.

The only way to fill that gap, to avoid mind-wandering, is to concentrate on what's being said. And that can be done by applying the rules I've already given you. *Get yourself involved* by self-questioning. That forces you to keep pace with the speaker.

Here are four specific ways to get involved....

1. *Summarize* what the speaker has already said. Try to boil it down to a single thought or two. Ask yourself, "How can I sum up these statements with one phrase or sentence? How do the statements tie in with the last point?" You're summarizing what has already been said. (And closing that time gap.)

2. *Anticipate* the speaker's next point with questions. "What exactly is the speaker reaching for here? What examples will be given to prove this point? Where will we go from here?" Ask the questions; anticipate the answers. You're forcing yourself to stay with the subject—maintaining attention.

3. *Between-the-lines-listening*. Try to find points that are not verbalized. Ask, "What is meant by that? Is the speaker hinting at something? Why isn't the obvious mentioned?" You are now listening between the lines.

4. Ask yourself if you *agree* with the speaker. "Is that statement correct? Isn't the speaker neglecting, or forgetting to mention so-and-so? Hasn't that situation changed?" You're asking yourself whether or not you agree.

Use these four rules to get yourself involved and you will most effectively negate mind-wandering. You'll leave yourself no choice but to pay attention—which is to *concentrate*. It's obvious, of course. You can't mentally *summarize* what the speaker has already said, *anticipate* what will be said, listen *between the lines*, and decide whether or not you *agree* with the speaker without really listening—or, again, without paying attention.

There is a mountainous island in the Caribbean called Saba. Remember *SABA* to help you remember Summarize, Anticipate, Between the lines, Agree.

Remember and apply the four rules (SABA) and you'll change listening from a passive to an active task. Their application will do away with mind-wandering, force you to keep your mind constantly and exclusively focused on the speaker's words and thoughts; and they'll help you to pull the core of meaning from the speech, talk, conversation, report, or lecture.

BONUS APPLICATION: ARITHMETIC CLUES

You've learned my techniques for remembering numbers of any length. Let's take a break—from trained-memory techniques, that is—so that I can show you some ways of *mentally* handling some arithmetic.

Break for Addition

Look at (don't try to solve) this addition problem:

$$
\begin{array}{r}
438 \\
274 \\
962 \\
883 \\
\underline{724} \\
\end{array}
$$

Assume that you need an exact total, an exact answer. But you have no paper, pencil, lipstick—no way to write. You have to do it in your head. How in the world would you go about doing that?

Try the *Elevator* System of adding!

$$438$$
$$274$$
$$962$$
$$883$$
$$\underline{724}$$

Put your finger on the 4 in the upper left corner (you won't need that finger after a while—you'll use eyes only) and take the "elevator" down with me—add *single digits only*, moving downward: 4, 6, 15, 23, 30. Are you with me? Nothing to it so far—you're adding *single digits*.

Now, take the elevator up with me. How? Look at the *single digit* to the right of your finger. You've just added the 7 at the bottom of the left column to reach 30. The digit to its right is a 2. Tack that 2 onto 30. *Don't add* it to 30—*tack it on*. Say to yourself: "302."

Now, going up, add single digits—and say the full answers to yourself: 302, 310, 316, 323, 326. You've just thought "three twenty-six."

Now, to the 326, *tack on* the digit to the right of the last digit you added. You've just said "three twenty-six"; tack on the 8, and say, "thirty-two sixty-eight" (3268).

Take the elevator down, the last time, adding single digits. Say each total to yourself (because you don't want to forget it). So: 3268, 3272, 3274, 3277, 3281.

You've stopped talking to yourself at "thirty-two eighty-one"—and that is the absolutely correct, *exact* answer!

Make up some addition problems and try it on your own. Before you know it, you'll run your eyes down, up, down—and have an exact answer. It's accurate and easy—because you're working with *single digits*!

You'll have that exact answer in seconds. The Elevator System will work as well for adding 4-digit numbers (down, up, down, up).

And there's more...

The Round-Off Approximation

Many business people I've taught this to tell me that it saves hours of their time. This system applies when you don't need an exact total (which you can arrive at via the Elevator System), but instead need a *fast* approximation.

Here's the rule: Each time you look at a number, *round it off* to its nearest hundred and then add the *single digit*. If the number is 50 or more, 150 or more, 350 or more, round it off to the next higher hundred. If the number is 49 or less, 149 or less, 349 or less, and so on, round it off to the next lower hundred.

Look at the numbers again:

$$438$$
$$274$$
$$962$$
$$883$$
$$\underline{724}$$

The first number, 438, "rounds off" to the next lower 100, or 400. Think 4. Continue: 4 + 3 (274 is 250 or more, so round off to 300) is 7, + 10 is 17, + 9 is 26, + 7 is 33. You know you're dealing with 100s, so think: 3300. You also know that the exact answer is 3281; you're off by only the merest percentage. Certainly a pretty good approximation, and it's done in *seconds*!

Try another one. Use the Round-Off Approximation first.

$$149$$
$$580$$
$$473$$
$$47$$
$$329$$
$$\underline{655}$$

Your mind could have worked like this: 1 (hundred) + 6 = 7; + 5 = 12 (the 47 is under 50, so forget it for now); +3 = 15; + 7 = 22, or 2200. If, as you went down the column, you skipped the 47, then glanced at the 329 and realized that the 47 brings it over 350 and used 4—it's okay. You'd have arrived at an approximation/estimate of 2300.

Now, use the Elevator System of adding to get an *exact* answer. See how close your approximation is.

Apply these ideas to *any* addition problem, including prices. Try it in the supermarket. Each time you drop an item into your shopping cart, round off its price and add those single digits. You'll have a "running" cost estimate!

Making Change

If you pay for a seventy-eight-cent item with a five-dollar bill, the cashier will "make change" by bringing each subtotal to *zero*. He or she will give you two pennies and say, "Seventy-eight and two is eighty..." then two dimes, "And twenty is one dollar..." then four one-dollar bills—"two, three, four, five dollars." The cashier made change by "piece work."

You can use that idea to mentally solve a formidable-looking problem like 43,255 + 8,324. Break down the smaller number to easy-to-add *zero-ending* numbers. "Change" 8,324 to 8,000, 300, 20, and 4.

Now the problem is 43,255 + 8,000. Well, that's easy. The answer, mentally, is 51,255.

And how much is 51,255 + 300? No problem! 51,555.

And how much is 51,555 + 20? 51,575, of course.

Finally, how much is 51,575 + 4?

The answer is 51,579!

Now so formidable after all, is it?

Break for Subtraction

Why bother switching on your computer, or calculator, or looking for pencil and paper to solve a subtraction problem like this one?

$$2650 \\ -\ 492$$

See if you can find an easy-to-add number to add to one of the vital numbers, bringing it to an easier-to-handle number, ending in zero or zeros, and add that amount to *both* numbers. For this problem add 8 to 492 to get 500. But remember that in subtraction, if you add the *same* number to *both* vital numbers, your answer remains correct. So, add 8 to 2650 also. The problem now looks like this:

$$2658 \\ -\ 500$$

This you can solve mentally: 2158!

361   Add 6 to each to get the zero: 367
− 54   − 60

Easy now ... the answer is 307.

There's more ...

$$\begin{array}{r} 847 \\ -558 \\ \hline \end{array}$$

You can take 47 *away* from the 847, to get 800.

But remember that you have to take the same 47 away from the 558—easy, of course—leaving you to work with 511. The problem is now easier to handle:

$$\begin{array}{r} 800 \\ -511 \\ \hline \end{array}$$

You can even break that down mentally. Instead of trying to take the 511 from the 800 in one fell swoop, take the 500 from 800 to get 300. There's still 11 to take away. Not a mindboggler. Take 11 from 300 and you get 289, the correct answer, which you arrived at without bringing a pencil near paper! (And if taking 11 from 300 *is* a problem for you, continue using "piece work." Take *10* from 300 to get 290, then take away the remaining 1, to arrive at 289.)

Final example: 814 minus 369 might throw you. But— add 1 to each to change the problem to 815 minus 370. Then, add 30 to each. The problem is now 845 minus 400. The answer, 445, is obvious.

I've touched on only a few of the ideas that will help you add and subtract mentally. But nothing worthwhile comes too easily. Put in some practice time—try the ideas, and apply them, on your own.

BONUS APPLICATION: COMPUTER PROGRAMS

In order to run your microcomputer, there are quite a few things you have to remember. If you're just starting to learn how to program, you'll want to remember the sequence of programs. As an example, one of the simplest programs is one that tells the computer to print the numbers from 1 to 10 on its screen and/or its printer. Only three commands are necessary:

```
10—For P = 1 to 10
20—Print P
30—Next P
```

The list, or line, numbers (10, 20, 30) are immaterial; you can use any ascending numbers. And the letter (P) could be any letter (or variable).

Form a simple Link to help you remember this "For-Next" loop. (A "next" must always follow a "For" in BASIC computer language. Visualize a golfer about to tee off—he yells "Fore!" He drives, then turns to his opponent and says, "Next.")

You might "see" a *pea* (P) teeing off, and yelling "Fore." (For P.) To represent equal, see it waving an American flag. (That's a standard I use. Americans are all *equal*, so I see an American flag to represent the equal sign.) See that flag wearing a large tie (1) which falls *to* (to) your *toes* (10). This "silly" Link will remind you of the first command:

For P = 1 to 10

Continue the Link: Associate *toes* to Print P. You might see a printing press between your toes, and it's printing only Ps.

See those printed Ps flying onto your *neck* (Next). Each time one does, you yell, "Next P."

Silly isn't it? That's the point! All you have to do is try it.

As you get more deeply involved in programming, you'll be lost in a morass of peeks, pokes, calls, ASCII character codes, and so on. Any of these can be memorized by applying my systems, and that will save you from much time and aggravation searching through your manuals.

For example, to command the computer to "wait for a keypress" (program stays on pause until any key is pressed) you'd use Call −756. (There are other ways. This is a subroutine.) I originally remembered that by seeing my computer come to a complete *halt* because it wanted to watch some *miners* clash. I always visualize a mynah bird or miners to represent (remind me of) the *minus* sign. Clash, of course, can only represent 756. (I knew that the command is *Call* −756, but if you want to be reminded of it, you can see your computer *calling* to the miners.)

Although you can simply type "inverse" to make your computer print black on white instead of white on black, "Call −384" will also do it. You can see yourself calling a mover to reverse your screen. To go back to normal, you can type "normal," but "Call −380" will also do it. I originally pictured movies that were white images on black screens.

I pictured myself calling a "tassle in" (or tusslin') to ring a gigantic bell in order to remember that the command "Call −1052" causes the computer to make a click (ring its bell) at that point in the program. ("Call −198" also rings the bell; a ringing bell is the tip off.)

Associating and remembering some, or all of these, will certainly save you a lot of time.

If you need to know ASCII character codes, then you're deeper into programming than I am, and you also know that most of the keys are pressed as you also hold down the *Ctrl* (control) key.

You can use the Alphabet Peg Words to remind you of the character name (which is composed of 2, 3, or 4 letters) or make up a word that will remind you of it. Example: An elevated train (L) is making an effort (F) not to go to jail (J). Or, you can turn left into jail. Either will remind you—once you decide which to use—of the character name LF and Ctrl J.

A naked man (or woman—NAK) is riding a female sheep, a ewe. Character name NAK—Ctrl U (which is the same as pressing the right-arrow key). You could, of course, have visualized a *hen* and an *ape* on a *cake*... on a ewe.

A *can* full of *eggs* will remind you of the character name—CAN—and Ctrl X.

A college *dean* is on an *el* (elevated train) with an *eel* and they're eating *peas*. Character name DLE—Ctrl P.

And so on...

I've given you only a few examples. Teaching you how to remember all the things you might want to remember about computer programming would take a book in itself. (Not a bad idea!)

But I've used these few examples to show you that it can be done, and to give you a general idea of how. You should be able to take it from here.

Making Your Own Bonus Applications

Obviously, I could list pages and pages of applications. That would be a waste of my space and your time. The systems are applicable to *any* memory problem. A few examples and case histories:

Do centigrade (Celsius) degrees confuse you? Instead of using a mathematical formula to make conversions to Fahrenheit, simply associate, for example, *law* to *rod* to tell you that 5 degrees centigrade is the same as 41 degrees Fahrenheit. *Towel* to *lip* tells you that 15 degrees centigrade is 59 degrees Fahrenheit.

One of my students lived in Copenhagen for a while. His favorite restaurant was known for its sandwich menu, which listed hundreds of sandwiches by number and looked like a roll of paper towels. He became a favorite customer because he used the memory systems to remember all the sandwich numbers. One example: Number 123 was a pickled herring sandwich. His association was of a pickled (drunk) herring dressed in <u>de</u><u>ni</u><u>m</u>.

Remembering playing cards is easy—if you make up a card word for each card in the deck, enabling you to visualize that ordinarily intangible card. Systematize it, of course. Example: let the first (letter) sound of the word represent the *value* (1 for ace through 13 for king); the last letter or sound represents the *suit* (*S* for spades; *H* for hearts, *D* for diamonds; and *K* or hard *C* for clubs). So, *joke* or *jock* could represent only the six of clubs. The "j" sound is 6, the "k" sound for clubs. *Times* could represent only the king of spades. T and m = 13, and the s represents spades. *Seed* = 10D, or ten of diamonds. There is no zero of any suit, so the "s" sound at the beginning of a word can represent 10. *Dash* = 1H, or ace of hearts. And so on.

When you come up with a card word for each of the 52 cards, you can then remember a shuffled deck in order. Associate your Peg Word to the card word. If the five of hearts is the twenty-seventh card, associate *lash* (1 = 5; H = hearts) to *neck*. As a demonstration, when a number is called (between 1 and 52), you'll know the card at that position. If a card is called, you'll know at what position it lies.

So, you'd like to win at Trivial Pursuit? Since it's *all* based on memory, no problem. As you play, apply the systems and memorize each answer. Visualize Clark Gable using a lawn *mower* to remind you that Clark Gable won the Academy Award for best actor in 1934. See a *cold beer* (Colbert) in the same picture to tell you that Claudette Colbert won for best actress. See it all *happening* in *one night*; include a *cap* (cheering "*rah!*") in your picture, and you'll know that the best movie that year was *It Happened One Night*, and the best dirctor was Frank (get a *frank*furter into your association if you feel you need it) Capra. You can memorize all the Academy Awards, or any trivia, this way.

A coin collector once wrote me: "How terrific! I made a Link of all the coins I needed—denomination, date, mint, etc.—and I never have to carry pieces of paper. When I find a coin store during a business trip, I *know* what to look for."

An accountant has to pass a stringent test before he can become a Certified Public Accountant. Basically, it's a memory test, as most tests are. For instance: If a client sells his primary residence, *how much* of the profit does he not have to pay taxes on if he's past *what* age? The answers are: $125,000 and 55 years of age. Michael B. told me that he had originally pictured himself selling a house but pulling a *tunnel* (125—he knew it was thousands) out of it first and putting it into his own pocket instead of the government's. His hand came out of his pocket with a *lily* (55); this told him the age.

Years ago, before off-track betting was legal, men with broken noses or cauliflower ears, usually wearing pin-striped suits (slight bulge at left armpit), black shirts, white ties, and usually named Duke, would approach me and say, "Listen, kid, I'm a doctor [!] and I need to learn how to remember names and numbers."

I taught some of these guys. (I was afraid not to.) They were bookies, and were always worried about being arrested. Their problem was to avoid getting caught with slips of paper listing the bets. They tried everything. One method that flourished for a while was to scratch the bets (names of bettors, horses, race numbers, track, and so forth) on a half dollar with a pin. If the bookie accidentally spent the coin—big trouble! So they started using my memory systems; then they couldn't get caught with any physical evidence. They were pretty good, too. They had to be, there was no leeway for mistakes. (The "Duke" I spoke to once about this said, "Don't mention my name, kid—or I'll break your memory!")

Last Few Words

So—you've read this far, nodding affirmatively all the way ("Oh, that's *right*; that'll work; gotta try that!"), but you haven't *tried* any of the techniques yet. Well then, you haven't accomplished anything, have you? You've wasted your time, and mine. Start again, will you? But *do* the things I ask you to do this time. Get yourself actively involved.

The goal I set for myself in writing this book was a simple one. To teach my ideas, systems, and techniques in a faster, more fun-filled, more to-the-point way than I've ever done before.

Too many examples, too much testing and drilling, are not necessarily good teaching devices. I believe that an interested reader/student will do his or her own testing and drilling when I suggest it, and even when I don't.

I've selected examples that, collectively, will show you the flexibility of the ideas and systems. If you understand that they can solve *any* memory problem with a slight (common sense) change here or there, then I've accomplished my purpose.

Each time you try an idea, you *have* to learn *something*.

Yes, a bit of effort is necessary to try the ideas. Do you know of *anything* worthwhile that can be acquired without at least a bit of effort? Even having fun requires some effort.

And learning my systems is *fun!*

ABOUT THE AUTHOR

HARRY LORAYNE is the author of ten previous books on memory, founder of the Harry Lorayne School of Memory, widely sought-after speaker and seminar leader, and he has demonstrated his astounding memory feats on virtually every major television talk show and in corporate meeting rooms across the country. His clients include scores of Fortune 500 companies, while thousands of graduates of his school attest to the power of his systems to transform their lives. His best-selling books have been translated into fourteen languages, and *The Memory Book* enjoyed nearly a year on *The New York Times* bestseller list. For his videotaped memory course he won an award for excellence in production at the International Film & TV Festival of New York.

Printed in the United States
by Baker & Taylor Publisher Services